Library of
Davidson College

James Pinckney Henderson
TEXAS' FIRST GOVERNOR

James Pinckney Henderson

TEXAS' FIRST GOVERNOR

by Robert Glenn Winchester

The Naylor Company
Book Publishers of the Southwest
San Antonio, Texas

Copyright ©, 1971 by THE NAYLOR COMPANY

This book or parts thereof may not be reproduced without writtten permission of the publisher except for customary privileges extended to the press and other reviewing agencies.

Library of Congress Catalog Card No. 70-143463

ALL RIGHTS RESERVED

Printed in the United States of America

ISBN 0-8111-0396-X

To my Mother

PREFACE

NEW ENGLAND has had a great advantage over the rest of the United States in publicizing its heroes and its great men. Developing early as a center of literature, culture, and book publishing, its poets, novelists, and historians spread over the nation and the world the stories of the brave deeds and accomplishments of its sons and daughters. In the meantime, the deeds of the great men of other sections went largely unsung and unheralded, except in their own localities.

Henry Sherman Boutelle spoke of this fact in an address at the University of North Carolina. Here is one sentence of his speech:

> Massachusetts, my native state, has furnished the nation with most of its heroes; not because North Carolina and the other states of the Old Thirteen had no heroes, but because Massachusetts had the poets.[1]

Millions of persons do not know that the first permanent English settlement at Jamestown, Va. preceded that in Massachusetts by thirteen years. Many historians think that the first shots of the American Revolution were fired at the Battle of the

Alamance in North Carolina several years before the "shot heard round the world" was fired at Lexington. Many North Carolinians believe that the first American Declaration of Independence was in Mecklenburg County, North Carolina, more than a year before the historic document was signed at Philadelphia in 1776.

With the possible exception of the colorful Sam Houston, most Texas heroes are relatively unknown outside the Lone Star State. One of these who is usually overlooked, even in Texas, is James Pinckney Henderson.

There is no Texan, with the possible exception of Houston, who had a more colorful and versatile career as lawyer, statesman, soldier, and diplomat than Henderson. There was no one of more value to the Republic and to the State of Texas. We will search in vain to find a public man of more honesty, integrity, humility, and unselfish service.

The histories of the United States, Mexico, Great Britain, and France would not be complete without a study of Henderson's actions that affected them. Neither would the histories of several other states in addition to Texas. It is truly extraordinary that his story has been largely neglected.

The writer's father was born and reared near Monroe, N.C., in Union County, which was formed from parts of Anson and Mecklenburg counties in 1842. On visits to this area as a boy, the writer heard many stories of early settlers in this area. All were strong in their opinion that Andrew Jackson was born in Mecklenburg County after his father's death on Twelve-Mile Creek in 1767. He was taken by his mother to a Mr. Crawford's in South Carolina shortly after birth, which accounts for the claim of South Carolina to be Old Hickory's birthplace.[2]

The author's great-grandfather married a member of the Houston family, some of whom resided in Union County. Her name was Nancy Houston; she was born in 1813, and died in 1897.[3]

Lincolnton, county seat of Lincoln County, N.C. and the birthplace of Henderson, is only about forty miles from Monroe. It is truly remarkable that Sam Houston, Andrew Jackson, and James Pinckney Henderson, who were to play such important roles in the future of Texas, should have spent their early lives in this general area.

The late Mrs. Boyce Henderson Wimberly, a collateral descendant of the first governor, resided in Yoakum and in Austin in her later years. She was the source for many valuable papers, letters, and other materials.

The writer is greatly indebted to the late Mrs. Frances Henderson Randall, grandniece of James P. Henderson of Lincolnton, N.C., to the late Dr. Archibald Henderson of the University of North Carolina at Chapel Hill, for material and suggestions of sources; to Dr. Edwin Novak, now of Ohio State University at Columbus, for checking sources at the University of Texas; and to Professor J. E. Conner, former chairman of the Department of History of the Texas College of Arts and Industries, for his valuable suggestions and help in finding material. Much of this material was used as part of the requirements for a master of arts degree in history at Texas A&I College.

I must not forget the late Dr. Henry T. Trantham, long-time professor of Greek and history at

Baylor University at Waco, a graduate of Wake-Forest College and a Rhodes Scholar, for his inspiration and the sharing of his immense knowledge of history during my undergraduate days.

Robert Glenn Winchester

---

1 Samuel Huntington Hobbs, *North Carolina Economic and Social*. Chapel Hill, N.C. The University of North Carolina Press, (1930) p. 220.

2 An affidavit, made by the author's great-great-grandfather, Thomas D. Winchester, Sr., in 1858, stated that his father, Douglas Winchester, rented the land later occupied by Andrew Jackson, Sr. on Twelve-Mile Creek, and later died there before the birth of his son. This is reproduced in *A Story of Union County and the History of Pleasant Grove Camp Ground* by George T. Winchester, (1937) privately printed at Mineral Springs, N.C.

3 The most famous member of the North Carolina branch of the Houston family was also closely aligned to Texas. This was David Franklin Houston, born in Monroe, Union County in 1866; died in 1940. He was a graduate of Harvard who has the distinction of being the only man to serve both as president of Texas A&M and The University of Texas. He was later Chancellor of Washington University of St. Louis, and also served as Secretary of Agriculture and as Secretary of the Treasury in Woodrow Wilson's cabinet.

CONTENTS

List of Illustrations		xiii
Chapter 1	Ancestry	1
Chapter 2	Birth and Early Life	9
Chapter 3	To Texas by Way of Mississippi	13
Chapter 4	Diplomatic Mission to Great Britain	21
Chapter 5	On the Continent	29
Chapter 6	Marriage and Return to Texas	49
Chapter 7	Election As First Governor of the Lone Star State	63
Chapter 8	Chief Executive and Major General of Texas Volunteers	77
Chapter 9	Closing Events of a Great Career	97
Chapter 10	Family Notes	103
Bibliography		106
Index		111

LIST OF ILLUSTRATIONS

Picture section between pages xiv and 1

Page 1 James Pinckney Henderson while Governor of Texas

Page 2 "Woodside," birthplace of James Pinckney Henderson, Lincolnton, N. C., built in 1800

Page 3 The Henderson family coat of arms

Page 4 James Pinckney Henderson while serving as Republic of Texas Minister to The Court of St. James's, London

James Pinckney Henderson while Governor of Texas

"Woodside," birthplace of James Pinckney Henderson, Lincolnton, N. C., built in 1800

The Henderson family coat of arms

Reprinted courtesy of Robert N. Randall, Mooresville, N. C.

James Pinckney Henderson while serving as Republic of Texas Minister to The Court of St. James's, London

Chapter 1

Ancestry

IF ANY PROOF were needed that heredity influences men's lives, one could find no better example than that of James Pinckney Henderson. Merely from studying his ancestry, one would expect him to cherish and fight for freedom and liberty, to open up new lands, to have a keen and searching intellect, and a character above reproach.

There is no doubt that the Henderson family came to America as a part of that vast emigration from Scotland in the eighteenth century.[1] After the final rebellion of the Scots had failed, and their chiefs had taken the oath of allegiance to the Queen, the lords gradually extinguished mortgages and leases and left thousands without land. The Highlands were overpopulated. As sheep growing began, thousands of farm laborers were evicted, and in 1770 competition from Ireland practically ruined the linen trade. Large landholders were victimized and robbed wholesale by those in poverty and want.

In 1772, James Hogg organized a group of 280 persons to accompany him to North Carolina. In the same year, from Sutherland and Strathaven, a ship sailed with 300 passengers, and another with 300 in 1773. Due to lawless conditions and large emigrations, many of the lords sold their estates and sailed to America. The number going from the Highlands to the New World from 1763 to 1775 is estimated at 20,000.[2]

There is no direct evidence that James Pinckney's forbears in Scotland were of the landed gentry, but there is reason to believe that they were. The fact that they became, almost at once, large landholders, town builders, lawyers, and office holders would seem to bear this out. Photographs taken in 1945 of the Fordell estate show an ancient castle and a mansion house which some of the present-day Henderson family believe to be the ancestral estate.[3]

The earliest known ancestor of James Pinckney was Samuel Henderson, who was born in 1700, married in 1733 and settled in North Carolina in 1740. He had eleven children: Mary, Richard, Nathaniel, Elizabeth, Ann, Susan, John, Samuel, William, Thomas, and Pleasant.[4] From these the various branches have developed.

Nearly all of the Scots who emigrated to America passed over the tidewater sections of Virginia and North Carolina for two reasons. One was that the land there was all taken up and laid out in large plantations. The other was that the Piedmont section was more like the Highlands of Scotland. The largest number had sailed from the northernmost counties of Sutherland and Caithness. However, there is reason to believe that James Pinckney's forbears sailed from Dumfries, in the extreme southern part of Scotland in the early seventeenth century and settled first in Virginia.[5]

James Pinckney Henderson was the son of Lawson Henderson and Elizabeth Carruth, and the grandson of James Henderson and Violet Lawson. Thus the future Texan was a great-grandson of Hugh Lawson, who emigrated to North Carolina about 1755. James Henderson lived in Rowan County, North Carolina, as did the Lawsons, and the name Lawson appears in both branches.[6]

James was said to be a strong patriot and supporter of the cause of independence. His son, Lawson, was a prominent citizen of Lincoln County, N.C., and held the office of clerk of the Superior Court for several years. He was the winner of the famous lawsuit of Hoke vs. Henderson, in which the United States Supreme Court held that an office is property, a decision that was reversed by the Court seventy years later by majority decision, with two justices dissenting. Lawson Henderson was spoken of as a "man of genuine ability, generous impulses, and deep piety." He was a Federalist in politics, and a warm friend of Charles Cotesworth and James Pinckney of South Carolina, for whom two of his sons were named.[7]

Worth S. Ray, of Austin, Texas, states that James, the grandfather of James P., was the son of William Henderson, who married a Miss Logan in Virginia. William's father was Thomas of New Kent

County in Virginia. Lawson, the father of the future governor of Texas, was a first cousin of the famous Judge Richard Henderson, organizer of the Transylvania Company.[8]

Among the leading men of Granville and Orange Counties were Richard Henderson and John Williams (his first cousin), along with Thomas and Nathaniel Hart, William Johnston, and John Luttrell of Chatham County. These men of affairs and broad vision were making plans for a huge real estate and colonizing scheme.[9]

The clerk of the county court at Salisbury, N.C., was Squire Boone. While appearing before his court in 1763, Richard Henderson met his son, Daniel, and listened to his tales of hunting and trapping in the western wilderness. These tales stimulated the imagination of the lawyer greatly. At that time the upper half of North Carolina extended to the mythical "South Sea," and was the property of the Earl of Granville.[10]

In 1763, the Richard Henderson Company was organized with John Williams and Thomas and Nathaniel Hart. It was later to develop into the Louisa Company and finally into the Transylvania Company. Boone and two companions were engaged to make a two-year confidential survey of the western lands, with a view to speculation and colonization of the trans-Allegheny region. Boone was also to investigate the possibility of securing leases or buying the lands that had been granted to the Cherokees in this area.[11]

Since Richard Henderson was appointed by Governor William Tryon as associate-justice of the highest court in North Carolina in 1768, and served until 1773, plans for the colonizing project were held in abeyance. In 1774, however, the Louisa Company was organized, succeeded by the Transylvania Company in 1775. The promoters of this bold scheme evidently aimed at a proprietary form of government in the new area.[12]

In the same year, a treaty was made with the whole tribe of the Cherokees, in which the company was granted twenty million acres of land at the Sycamore Shoals of the Watauga River. Daniel Boone and a corps of axemen cut the trail and settlement began.[13]

A detailed story of the Transylvania story is not in order here, but it is interesting to note that Richard Henderson and John Williams, his cousin, were elected by the Transylvania Legislature at Boonesboro as delegates to the Continental Congress at Philadelphia in September, 1775, though they were not seated. John Adams was still a loyalist and considered Henderson and associates "dangerously independent and republican."[14]

Thomas Jefferson later recommended that Virginia recognize this new colony at her back door. The Virginia Convention was asked to recognize the Cherokee grant, but instead confiscated the purchase and created from it the County of Kentucky. The company was granted 200,000 acres between the Green and Ohio Rivers by Virginia in 1778 by way of compensation. Judge Henderson then started a settlement at French Lick (later Nashville, Tenn.) in 1780. This was eventually taken over by North Carolina, but the company was later compensated with a grant of 200,000 acres.[15]

Thus we see that it was no departure from tradition for young James Pinckney Henderson to move to new lands in Mississippi and Texas and to take an active part in their public affairs and early struggles. His ancestors in Scotland and North Carolina had pointed the way. Thus it is that we find a Henderson County in North Carolina, Kentucky, Tennessee, and Texas, and towns bearing the Henderson name in the Tar Heel State and in Texas. The future governor's kinsmen were opening up that great arc of settlement that poured emigrants into Texas to "fight for their rights" and maintain the Lone Star Republic.

James T. De Shields makes this comment:

> By birth and inherited traits and traditions, Governor Henderson belonged distinctly to what John Randolph called "the wealthy and well-born" . . . He came of a family of distinguished lawyers and statesmen, orators and soldiers — men in whom the love of learning was an instinct; who practiced law for the sheer pleasure of its glorious contests and its profound principles of justice and philosophy; who followed politics for the exhiliarating excitement of the game, and adopted statesmanship as a calling for the benevolence of its objects and the satisfaction of its achievements.[16]

---

[1] Archibald Henderson, "The Transylvania Company: A Study in Personnel; I. James Hogg," *Tilson Club Historical Quarterly*, XXI, No. 1, (January, 1947), pp. 4-6. Hereafter referred to as A. Henderson, "Transylvania Co. I."

[2] *Ibid.*, p. 7.

[3] These photographs were secured by the late Horace Wimberly, Jr., an attorney of Austin, Texas, while he was on duty with the U.S. Armed Forces in the British Isles in 1945.

[4] Lucy Henderson Horton, *The Horton Family* (Franklin, Tenn. Publisher not known, 1922) This data is from a copy. The book itself was not seen.

[5] Archibald Henderson, "Two Tar Heels Played Leading Role in

Welding Texas to American Union," *Daily News*, (Greensboro, N. C. April 22, 1928). Hereafter referred to as A. Henderson, "Two Tar Heels."
6 *Ibid.*
7 *Ibid.*
8 Worth S. Ray, "Information on J. Pinckney Henderson," *Southwestern Historical Quarterly*, XLIX (Oct., 1945), p. 301.
9 A. Henderson, "Transylvania Co. I," p. 9.
10 *Ibid.*, p. 9.
11 *Ibid.*, p. 10.
12 *Ibid.*, p. 10-11.
13 *Ibid.*, pp. 11-12.
14 *Ibid.*, pp. 12-13.
15 *Ibid.*, pp. 14-17.
16 James T. De Shields, *They Sat in High Place* (San Antonio, Texas: The Naylor Company, 1940), pp. 165-166. Hereinafter referred to as De Shields, *High Place*.

Chapter 2
Birth and Early Life

JAMES PINCKNEY, son of Lawson Henderson and Elizabeth Carruth Henderson, was born at Lincolnton, Lincoln County, North Carolina, on March 31, 1808. His birthplace is still standing, in good condition, about two miles from Lincolnton.[1] His early years were exciting times for the new nation. The Federal Constitution had been in operation only a short time, and the people of the United States were struggling to maintain it and gain a place for the new country among the nations of the world. Growing up as he did among lawyers, politicians, and men of affairs, young Henderson must have learned a great deal of the significance of these stirring events. He could not then realize that he was later to assist at the birth of two new constitutions, to play a vital part in maintaining a new republic among the nations, and in finally adding a Lone Star to the Star-Spangled Banner.

As for his parents, Lawson Henderson was a prominent member of the Federalist Party, and was active in local and state affairs. J. Pinckney later told his associates in Texas that he had a very strong affection for his mother. She once stated, when asked if he had ever been refractory: "No, some of my other boys were headstrong, but Pinckney was always a good boy."[2]

Early associates have said that J. Pinckney never had a strong constitution, and had early symptoms of tuberculosis. His face was said to be handsome and intellectual and his portraits as a young man bear this out. It was also asserted that the voice of the future statesman and diplomat was musical, flexible and magnetic.[3] This is also borne out by later evidence. There is no doubt that he inherited in full measure the Scot's love of learning and his industriousness, as he almost ruined his health by furious application to his studies.

Henderson's early education was obtained at Pleasant Retreat Academy in Lincolnton.[4] He continued his studies at the old Chapel Hill College. Many distinguished Southerners received their education here, as it was noted for "literary and scientific culture." Henderson's adoption of the law as his profession was due to "his inherited estate and the customs of his class."[5]

In the *Western Carolinian* for June 30, 1829, he was listed as having received his license to practice by the Supreme Court of North Carolina that month.

He had just turned twenty-one. Those listed with him were Joseph Caldwell of Iredell, N.C., Thomas J. Oakes of Rowan, N.C., Daniel M. Barringer of Cabarrus, N.C., and William B. Haskell of Pennsylvania. By studying the law eighteen out of twenty-four hours a day, Henderson permanently injured his health, which was already none too robust.[6]

At the age of twenty-two, the future major general was appointed as aide to General A. McDowell of the Fifth Division of the North Carolina State Militia, and later rose to the rank of colonel of militia.[7]

In the early days of his legal practice, Henderson was intimate with Ashbel Smith, then a resident of Salisbury, N.C. The future great statesman and citizen of Texas had come to Salisbury to study law after his graduation at Yale, but gave it up after one year, stating that he found it so absorbing that it was ruining his health. He certainly had this tendency in common with Henderson. Ashbel Smith, a native of Hartford, Connecticut, had been the guardian at Yale of Archibald Henderson, grandfather of Dr. Archibald Henderson of the University of North Carolina. Smith later studied medicine in New York, at Yale, and in Paris and still later followed Henderson to Texas.[8] Thus a contact made in the ivy-covered halls of a New England college led to the raw, crude frontier and to participation in the birth of a new nation and a new state.

---

[1] This information is from Mrs. Frances Henderson Randall, now deceased, sole member of the Henderson family who was still residing in the Lincolnton area in 1952. She was the grandniece of James Pinckney and the granddaughter of Charles Cotesworth Henderson, his brother.

[2] F. B. Sexton, "J. Pinckney Henderson," *The Quarterly of the Texas State Historical Association*, I (January, 1898), p. 189. This is a memorial

address delivered at ceremonies in honor of General Henderson at San Augustine, Texas, Aug. 21, 1858. Hereinafter referred to as Sexton, "J. Pinckney Henderson."

3 De Shields, *High Place*, p. 167.

4 This information is from the book, *Annals of Lincoln County, North Carolina*, by William L. Sherrill. Mrs. C. H. Sides of Statesville, N.C., sent me this and other information from her copy of the book.

5 De Shields, *High Place*, p. 166.

6 A. Henderson, "Two Tar Heels."

7 *Ibid*. Sexton and Lynch give the name of Pinckney's commanding officer as Major General A. McDorrett. Dr. A. Henderson is probably correct.

8 *Ibid*.

Chapter 3

To Texas by Way of Mississippi

THOUGH HENDERSON could count on a brilliant legal and political career in his home state, he determined to seek a warmer climate for the sake of his health. Therefore in 1835, at the age of twenty-seven, he moved to Canton, Madison County, Mississippi and set up a legal practice there. His education and legal training, as well as his oratorical ability, were so outstanding that he took a place immediately among the leading men of this area.[1]

At this time the topic of discussion on everybody's lips throughout the nation and especially in the South, was the situation in Texas. The largest part of the early settlers of Texas were from the South, and most of the men massacred at Goliad were sons of the leading Southern families, especially those of Georgia.

The plight of Texas and its brave fight for independence greatly aroused the sympathies of the young lawyer recently arrived in Canton. He made an impassioned appeal for aid for Texas at a mass meeting in 1836. Here he greatly impressed United States Senator Foote of Mississippi, who was a member of the audience. On asking who the brilliant young speaker was, the Senator was told that this was a Mr. Henderson, "a young lawyer of uncommon promise and of easy fortune from North Carolina, who had just settled among us." Large sums were quickly collected and a company was organized at once to go to the defense of Texas. Senator Foote, in describing young Henderson's oratorical powers, had this to say about him:

> His appearance was noble and commanding; his eyes and whole countenance flashed forth the light of commingling thought and passion, and he swept the audience before him like a whirlwind.[2]

A military company of about five hundred men was quickly raised and equipped, but Henderson went on ahead to Texas and reported to Provisional President David G. Burnet. He was at once appointed a Brigadier General of the Texas army and commissioned to return at once to the United States to raise additional forces. He hurried back to North Carolina and raised a company, which went to Texas under the command of John B. Harry, but, like the military unit from Mississippi, arrived after the battle of

San Jacinto. This North Carolina company was transported to Texas at the personal expense of Henderson.³

The new Texas Republic to which Henderson returned was in a chaotic and disorganized state. Houston found it necessary to go to New Orleans for medical treatment for the wound he had suffered at San Jacinto. Most of the early settlers who had fought for Texas independence had returned home to rebuild their homes and plant their crops. New volunteers kept pouring into Texas thirsting for action and maddened by the thought that they had arrived too late for glory on the battlefield. The men were stirred up by false rumors of a new invasion of Texas by Mexico, and, being idle and impatient of discipline, became a menace to the government.⁴

Two treaties had been signed with Santa Anna, one of which had provided for ending hostilities and the return of the dictator to Vera Cruz where he was supposed to work for Mexico's recognition of Texas independence. Two cabinet members had refused to sign the treaties, but nevertheless President Burnet hustled the Mexican Napoleon on board the Texas warship, *Invincible*, at Velasco to carry him to Mexico. As it prepared to sail, the steamer *Ocean* arrived with two hundred fifty men under command of Thomas Jefferson Green and dragged Santa Anna ashore in irons, in defiance of the government.⁵

Thomas J. Green and Memucan Hunt of North Carolina and Felix Huston, a swashbuckler from Mississippi, led the violent outcry for the immediate execution of Santa Anna, though Houston and other cooler heads realized that, once executed, he would be merely another dead Mexican that could do Texas no good. As well balanced and sane a man as Henderson was not exempt from this popular outcry. It is the only recorded instance of his being swayed by popular clamor instead of calm, reasoned judgment.[6]

The government was compelled to yield to the strong feelings of the army, and Santa Anna was sent under guard to the plantation of Dr. Orlando Phelps at Orizimbo on the Brazos. The treaties were later repudiated by the Mexican government, but Santa Anna was allowed to go to the United States and home to Mexico.

As a citizen of the new Republic, Henderson set up a law practice at Nacogdoches with General Thomas J. Rusk and Kenneth L. Anderson, the latter having recently arrived from North Carolina. This new firm quickly became one of the leading legal organizations of Texas. All of these men took a prominent part in the formation and administration of the policies of the Texas Republic.[7]

The oldest citizens had been in Texas only a few years, and many of the ablest were comparative newcomers. Recent arrival was no bar to distinction in the new government. Less than six months after coming to Texas, Henderson was made Attorney General. Houston had been elected President, and was organizing the government. James Collinsworth was offered the appointment, but declined. We find the nomination of Henderson among the archives of the new Republic:

Executive Department
Columbia, November 24, 1836
To the Honorable
The Senate

Gentlemen:

I have now the honor to present to you the name of J. Pinckney Henderson, Esquire, as an individual possessing moral worth, genius and talents proper to the discharge of the duties of that office . . .

Sam Houston[8]

The nomination was speedily confirmed on November 26. De Shields says that Henderson entered on this office in October, but, if so, it must have been an interim appointment, as the Senate was not given the nomination until November.[9] A hint of the financial difficulties involved in organizing the government departments is shown by this quote from *The Raven*:

James Pinckney Henderson, the good-looking and gay young Attorney-General, and Robert Barr, the Postmaster General, organized their departments on credit.[10]

However, Henderson was to hold his first office only briefly. A new position, of much greater importance, was to open the way for the greatest service to his adopted country.

Stephen F. Austin, the beloved "Father of Texas," had been named Secretary of State in Houston's cabinet, but his health was not good, and a chill brought on by his work in his unheated office res-

17

ulted in his death on December 27, 1836. Henderson was immediately appointed to the position and took over the tangled problems of Texas foreign policy.[11] The Republic's foreign problems were indeed formidable. It was forced to seek loans for its perpetually embarrassed treasury from the United States and European powers, at a time of financial stringency. Annexation to the Union, which seemed so inevitable after San Jacinto, ran into many difficulties. It was opposed by many influential Texans, including Lamar, and by the anti-slavery element of the North. The borders of Texas were unsettled, and sporadic invasions of Mexican forces kept alive the fear that Mexico would attempt to recapture her lost province. There was certainly not much hope of recognition of Texas independence by those defeated at San Jacinto. The Indians were a problem. Recognition by foreign powers was necessary and desirable, along with commercial treaties that would aid in building foreign trade. These were a few of the problems that absorbed the attention of the young secretary of state in the brief time that he held this important office.

---

[1] De Shields, *High Place*, p. 167

[2] A. Henderson, "Two Tar Heels." Also see De Shields, *High Place*, p. 167, Sexton, *J. Pinckney Henderson*, pp. 189-190.

[3] James Lynch, *Bench and Bar of Texas*. (St. Louis: Nixon Jones Publishing Company, 1885), p. 186. Also see A. Henderson, "Two Tar Heels."

[4] De Shields, *High Place*, p. 36. Also see Marquis James, *The Raven* (New York City: Blue Ribbon Books, Inc., 1929), pp. 269-270.

[5] James, *The Raven*, pp. 259-260. Also see De Shields, *High Place*, p. 37.

[6] De Shields, *High Place*, p. 37.

[7] *Ibid.*, p. 167.

[8] *Secret Journals of the Senate, Republic of Texas, 1836-1845* (Austin, Texas: Austin Printing Co., 1911), p. 24.

9 De Shields, *High Place*, p. 168. Also see *Secret Journals*, p. 24, for confirmation.

10 James, *The Raven*, p. 271.

11 Joseph William Schmitz, *Texan Statecraft, 1836-1845* (San Antonio: The Naylor Company, 1941), p. 38. Hereinafter referred to as J. W. Schmitz, *Texan Statecraft*. Also *Secret Journals*, p. 42, for nomination message, May 10, 1837, and p. 54 for confirmation by the Senate on May 22, 1837.

Chapter 4

Diplomatic Mission to Great Britain

THERE IS no doubt that the public men of the Republic of Texas were among the ablest on the North American continent. Yet James Pinckney Henderson at the age of twenty-nine was chosen for the vital mission to Europe to secure recognition from the Old World powers. Dr. Archibald Henderson has this comment:

> To this great compliment — at once to youth, to ability, to diplomatic qualities, to knowledge, and to wisdom — American history, I believe, offers no parallel.[1]

Due to the straitened condition of Texas finances, it was quite an advantage that Henderson was able to pay most of his own expenses. So, in the spring of 1837, he sailed with his credentials for the Courts of St. James's and St. Cloud. Memucan Hunt had resigned as Texan Minister at Washington, D.C., mainly because his hotel credit had run out; and Anson Jones succeeded him. Jones secured the confidence of a member of the United States diplomatic corps. This man stretched the diplomatic proprieties a great deal to write to Lord Palmerston, then the British Secretary for Foreign Affairs. In his letter he called attention to the increasing importance of Texas, and asked if it would not be desirable for Great Britain to have a friend on this continent. A memorandum of the great British diplomat of this period states in part: "The subject . . . is important."[2]

Even before annexation efforts had foundered on the rocks of the slavery controversy, Texas had started negotiations with England and France. This action had been recommended by Provisional-President David G. Burnet and also by the Committee on Foreign Relations of the First Texas Congress in November of 1836. It was often discussed. So it was no new policy when Henderson was sent to Europe in 1837 as agent and minister plenipotentiary to Great Britain and France. As agent, his duty was to secure recognition and then to begin preliminary negotiations for a commercial treaty.[3]

As the twenty-nine year old diplomat boarded one of the small ocean steamers that made the Atlantic run in that day, and settled down for the voyage, he may have thought of his ancestors who had made the trip in the other direction some hundred years before. If he felt any trepidation at the thought of a young man from a North Carolina small town and lately from the wilds of Texas negotiating with the suave, clever, polished, and experienced diplomats of the greatest world powers, he showed no sign of it in his correspondence, nor did any of his associates. He more than held his own in the splendid halls of Whitehall, Versailles and St. Cloud.

If one may digress a moment, it is perhaps worth stating that his very simplicity, earnestness, and lack of bombast were assets greatly to his advantage. His letters, writings, and speeches were markedly free of the flamboyance and extravagance of phrase that characterized most of the contemporary public men of his time. His simple, spare, clear style of writing is much different from that of Sam Houston, Mirabeau B. Lamar, and James Hamilton; to name a few examples. Henderson was a genuinely humble and modest man, and we need read no eulogies to discover it. It shows clearly in all that he wrote and spoke. Such qualities would appeal to the British, and to the French; they had the charm of novelty. Memories of Benjamin Franklin were still green in France.

Great Britain had reason to be interested in Texas. Her interest was based on her traditional policy of supporting Mexico against the United States. This had begun with Canning as early as 1825, and had been followed since then by British foreign ministers. A very important item was that of commercial interests in Mexico and a valuable Mexican trade. Also a large part of the Mexican national debt was held by British bondholders. As for Texas independence, the English looked for reconquest of the area at an early date. They were strongly opposed to its annexation to the United States because of the commercial advantages that would be thus gained over Great Britain. Finally, the British wished to prevent, if possible, the extension of slavery into Texas.[4]

Henderson arrived in London early in October of 1837, and almost at once opened negotiations with Lord Palmerston. He found that the British Foreign Office was not actively interested in a treaty with Texas. On the contrary, Palmerston was inclined to uphold the traditional policy, mentioned above, of supporting Mexico as a barrier against the United States. After a series of conferences, the Foreign Minister placed the matter before the Cabinet and its decision was placed before Henderson on December 27, 1837. England was to delay recognition. The reason given was doubt that Texas could maintain its independence. Henderson reported to Irion, Texas Secretary of State, that the real reasons were: the slavery issue, which would arouse controversy in England, English creditors' interests in Mexico, and uncertainty about annexation. Due to the difficulties mentioned, he would go to France, where more favorable conditions existed.[5]

Since slavery played such a strong part in the negotiations with England, it might be of interest to look at some of its aspects. A strong abolitionist element existed in England, and O'Connell, an opposition leader in Parliament, put pressure on the Government to oppose all compromises with slavery. A World's Convention of Abolitionists was held in London in 1843, which some Americans attended, and in which the abolition of slavery was discussed.[7] As usual, English commercial interest was aligned with her idealism. The British had recently freed the slaves of the West Indies, temporarily placing Britain at a disadvantage with the United States, where the agricultural South still maintained slavery. The extension of slavery into Texas, and its annexation by the United States were to be prevented on both moral and practical grounds. Many men of vision in the South could see in their minds a United South, and Texas with a separate government.[8] Indeed, Sam Houston wrote a letter to General Murphy in 1844, in which he outlined a Republic of Texas extending from lower Oregon down into Lower California and Chihuahua, and taking in all the southern states.[9] Houston probably was only trying to prod the United States into action on annexation, but there were many in the South and in Texas who were in deadly earnest about similar schemes.

England's wish then was to persuade Texas to remain independent and to free its slaves. Therefore, it exerted pressure on the Republic to emancipate its Negroes as a price for recognition.[10] This was one of the greatest barriers that Henderson and others had to face in their diplomacy in England.

Before leaving for France, Henderson suggested that the two countries agree to a convention establishing commercial trade with Texas, but not committing the British to recognition. News of the probable withdrawal of Texas' annexation offer strengthened Henderson's hand, and he made an offer on the basis of the permanent independence of Texas. He received instructions from Irion, the Secretary of State, to press for: a commercial treaty, a defensive treaty against Mexico, or a loan. Texas would make mutual concessions with England in any agreement made. Palmerston submitted these propositions to the Board of Trade. They were accepted after long delay, Henderson showing his impatience by frequent notes asking for action.[11] This was an example of the persistence of the young diplomat in all his negotiations. There is evidence that it sometimes annoyed the deliberate and formal Palmerston, but the man who had studied law for eighteen hours a day continued his constant activity and persistence in all his diplomatic career.

The commercial arrangement finally signed was one of the most peculiar in the annals of diplomacy. England would still regard Texas as legally a part of Mexico but would trade with her as an independent nation. Texas would make out clearance papers for its ships as an independent country, and the British would "shut their eyes" to the circumstances of their having "Texian" papers. The arrangement was to be changed only if Great Britain or Mexico recognized the independence of the Texas Republic. President Houston proclaimed this arrangement on July 4, 1838.[12]

Henderson did not secure the recognition of Texas or the regular treaty of amity and commerce that he sought so diligently, but he prepared the ground and left the seed for later germination. He had done as well as could be expected against the powerful traditional policies of the Foreign Office and her many contrary interests in Mexico, as well as against the problem of slavery.

Henderson had one more proposal to make before leaving England. He asked that he be allowed to leave his secretary, George McIntosh, in England as his representative to keep in touch with the British

Foreign Office, in case there was a chance of further discussions. Palmerston, however, did not approve. He had had "enough importunity on the subject," but gave Henderson a letter to the Earl of Granville, the British minister to France, who would be able to inform the Texan of any further development of Foreign Office policy on recognition.[13]

---

1 A. Henderson, "Two Tar Heels." See *Secret Journals*, p. 58, for nominating message by Houston on May 29, 1837.

2 Marquis James, *The Raven*, p. 288.

3 J. W. Schmitz, *Texan Statecraft*, pp. 63-64. Another influence on sending a representative to Europe was that of Memucan Hunt, while he was Minister to the United States. He wrote many letters to Texas officials stressing the importance of negotiations for recognition and commercial treaties with England and France as a prod to the United States to forget sectional differences and admit Texas as a state. He thought the Southern States would never permit a foreign power to gain influence over territory so important to their economy. *Ibid.*, pp. 56-57.

4 Ephraim Douglass Adams, *British Interests and Activities in Texas* (Baltimore: The Johns Hopkins Press, 1910), pp. 15-17. Hereinafter referred to as: Adams, *British Interests*. See also J. W. Schmitz, *Texan Statecraft*, p. 64.

5 J. W. Schmitz, *Texan Statecraft*, p. 64.

6 *Ibid.*, p. 142. James Hamilton in 1840 wrote of this difficulty. He was convinced it was a major obstacle to recognition.

7 *Ibid.*, pp. 200-201.

8 Marquis James, *The Raven*, p. 342.

9 *Ibid.*, p. 350.

10 *Ibid.*, p. 342.

11 J. W. Schmitz, *Texan Statecraft*, p. 65.

12 *Ibid.*, p. 66. Also Adams, *British Interests*, p. 20.

13 J. W. Schmitz, *Texan Statecraft*, p. 66.

Chapter 5

On the Continent

HENDERSON CONSIDERED that he would have a much better chance to secure recognition and treaties of amity and commerce from France than he had from England for several reasons. There would be no trouble over the slavery issue. No Mexican bonds were held by the French. France had no colony which might seek independence, as Texas had done, and there was no powerful political party which might seize any opportunity to criticize the government and create trouble, as there was in England.[1]

The Texan commissioner was to find, however, that France was to be entangled in difficulties with Mexico, and that these troubles were to delay and to complicate his negotiations. The French had made a provisional arrangement with Mexico in 1827, but it was never signed. The many revolutions in Mexico, the unstable governments, and unsettled conditions throughout the country had brought damage to property of French citizens. Claims for damages had not been paid, and on January 16, 1838, the French diplomatic representative, Baron de Defandis, withdrew from Mexico. Damages for $600,000 were fixed by the French, and other demands were made on the Mexican government. On April 16, diplomatic relations were suspended and a blockade of Mexican ports was begun.[2]

Negotiations for a settlement failed, and as a result, the French squadron bombarded San Juan de Ulua, reducing it in a short time. The Mexican forces were then badly defeated at Vera Cruz, Santa Anna losing a leg in this battle. Pakenham, the British minister to Mexico, offered mediation because of interference of the blockade with England's trade. His offices were accepted, and a convention and treaty were signed on March 9, 1839, allowing damages of $600,000 to be paid to French citizens.[3]

This, then, was the background of the French-Mexican difficulties that increased Henderson's problems of negotiation. He arrived in Paris on March 23, 1838, and the French government was officially notified of his arrival and desire to negotiate on April 28. Count Molé, French Minister of Foreign Affairs, was asked for a date on which Henderson could pay his respects.[4] Henderson felt, however, that the time was not favorable for starting conversations, unless the French difficulties with Mexico could be settled.[5] On May 26, Henderson asked for an interview during the blockade of Mexican ports by the French fleet. He reminded Molé that the United States had recognized Texas as a sovereign and independent nation, and had treated her as such for the past twelve months.[6]

The Foreign Minister met the Texan on May 31, 1838, though he pompously refused to receive Henderson as the "accredited agent of Texas," giving as his reason that to do so might be construed as partial recognition of her independence. After he was assured that this reception would not be considered that way, Molé consented to an informal discussion. Henderson, however, did show his credentials.[7]

Since the interpreter was so poor, the interview did not go very well, and the Texas agent asked permission to submit a letter setting forth the case of Texas. This was granted, and the letter was submitted on June 1. In this important communication, Henderson showed his diplomatic genius and his skilled attorney's pleading. He began by stating that Texas was a nation *de jure* as well as *de facto*. A short account of the settlement of Texas was given, along with the conditions that led to independence. The grant to Moses Austin in 1821 by the King of Spain, and the special colonial laws of 1823, 1824, and 1825 were shown as inducements to settlers to Texas. Under the Mexican Federal Republic of 1824, Texas was assured that when it had a sufficient number of inhabitants, it might become a separate state, with all the privileges and rights of the others. When, in 1833, the required number had been secured, a petition was sent to the national Congress asking for separate statehood. The petition was ignored and the Texas agent thrown in jail.[8]

Santa Anna's usurpation, Henderson continued, had resulted in the overthrow of the constitution of

1824, and the setting up of a dictatorship; a centralized military government. Both Texas and Coahuila remonstrated, but General Cos was sent to compel obedience to the dictator. Thus the people of Texas, as well as many in Mexico, were roused to arms. A meeting in November of 1835 passed a resolution to restore the Constitution of 1824, and appealed to liberty-loving Mexicans to assist in the effort. The Texas Revolution, and the defeat of Santa Anna at San Jacinto, as well as his capture on April 21, 1836, resulted in a treaty signed by him agreeing to the removal of the Mexican Army from Texas. The dictator also agreed to use his influence to secure Mexico's recognition of Texas independence that had been declared on March 2. The Mexican Congress had repudiated the treaty, the letter continued, and had announced its intention of subduing Texas, but after two years no serious attempt to do so had been attempted. Texas was fully capable of maintaining her independence. Mexico had exhausted her resources, while Texas had grown in population and wealth; of an area of two hundred million acres, only thirty million were settled; the remaining domain was the property of the State and would yield great revenue.[9]

Henderson, well knowing that diplomatic ends are usually secured by appealing to the self-interest of the opposite nation, then played on the theme of the advantage to France of a commercial treaty and recognition. Knowing that France was interested in cheap cotton for her textile mills, he called attention to the high tariff of the United States. He stated that sugar, rice, and indigo could be grown easily, that Texas would never be a manufacturing country, and would find it desirable to admit French wines, silks, and fine cotton goods on fair terms. He also mentioned Texas' ability to produce naval stores.[10]

Henderson then took up a serious stumbling-block to recognition and the negotiation of commercial treaties — that of the possibility of annexation of Texas by the United States. He stated that, though it was true that most of the citizens of Texas had desired annexation soon after separation from Mexico, her advances had been rejected, and consequently it was no longer desired. Texas now felt secure against any attempt at reconquest. The Republic was an agricultural state and would be hurt economically by the imposition of the United States tariff, which would be imposed if it became a state. The United States, however, had recognized the independence of Texas, which was in a similar position to that of France in the July revolution that put Louis Phillipe on the throne.[11]

Thus ended Henderson's letter. It has been summarized at great length because it contains most of the arguments used throughout the negotiations. It was a masterly presentation, and undoubtedly had great effect, but many headaches were yet in store for the Texas agent, not all of them caused by Frenchmen.

A letter from Irion, Secretary of State, to Henderson, told of attempted smuggling of goods through Texas into Mexico to evade the French blockade previously mentioned. Corpus Christi was the port used most by the smugglers. The Texas government was afraid that France would think Texas was conniving with this smuggling, and, therefore, Henderson was instructed by the President to request France to extend her blockade to Texas.[12]

Henderson's reaction was strongly negative to

this suggestion, as he indicated in his letters to Irion. He had emphasized to the French Foreign Office the ability of Texas to maintain her independence and protect herself; if she now called on France to prevent smuggling through Texas, this contention would go out the window. It was true that a band of Mexicans had occupied Corpus Christi, but at the approach of a Texas force they had sailed for Matamoros. Therefore, Henderson decided not to mention the President's request to the French government unless he received further instructions. Since these were not forthcoming, nothing more was done about the matter.[13]

Henderson now believed that there was small chance for an agreement with France unless there were hostilities between France and Mexico. In the middle of August, there were rumors of a settlement between the two countries. Therefore, the Texan again put forward his claims for recognition, mentioning the fact that Texas had been independent for three years and had been recognized by the United States for eighteen months. In order to spur on negotiations, he hinted that he might soon leave France on another mission. Shortly thereafter, a conference with Molé was arranged and Henderson found out at least one of the reasons for the delay. He was informed that Alphonse de Saligny, one of the secretaries to the French Embassy in Washington, D.C., had been sent to Texas and was to make a report on the country. Therefore, no definite steps could be taken until this report had been received. This was Henderson's first notice of the little Frenchman, once spoken of by a Texas journalist as "a little whipper-snapper," who was to cause him and the Texas government so much trouble.[14]

Molé was reminded that England had not formally recognized Texas but had the subject under consideration and had signed a commercial agreement to open direct trade with the Republic. The Foreign Minister then asked when Henderson expected to leave France. The reply was that he was willing to stay all winter if there was any chance for a treaty, but he would like to leave in November. Molé then said that he doubted that a reply could be received from the French agent (Saligny) within two months.[15]

Henderson was as persistent in France as he had been in England. He was not willing to wait for Saligny's report without an attempt to secure at least a commercial arrangement. On October 1, 1838, therefore, he made a formal proposal for a commercial treaty. In it he stated that a country had, under international law, a right to make commercial arrangements with states that had revolted, before formal recognition of that state. The United States had made such an arrangement with Texas before its recognition. The main question for France was whether or not such an arrangement was expedient. Its advantages were again pointed out. Henderson requested that Texas vessels be allowed to enter French ports in accordance with French law, and French ships would be allowed in Texas ports on a most-favored-nation basis. Molé was favorable, and submitted the proposal to his government, which approved. Therefore, Henderson, since he had plenary powers, signed for Texas. He was pleased with this agreement, superior to that with England, which country still looked on Texas as a part of Mexico. Now, for the first time, a European power "recognized Texas as a nation and her authorities as a government."[16]

Henderson wrote to president-elect Lamar on November 14, 1838, giving the terms and explaining the commercial arrangement with France. The core of the agreement is contained in the following quotation:

> Until the mutual relations of Texas and France are regulated in a complete and definite manner, the citizens, the vessels, and the merchandize of the two countries shall enjoy in every respect in each of the countries the treatment accorded or which may eventually be accorded to the most favored nation, comformably moreover to the respective usages.

Stating further in the letter that he has received information that Anson Jones, Texas Minister at Washington, D.C., had withdrawn the offer of annexation. Henderson expressed the belief that this would aid his negotiations for recognition from France. Continuing, he said that many crews on English ships were made up of free Negroes and Mulattoes and suggested that all future treaties made by Texas should contain a provision that no ships with free Negroes should be allowed into ports of the Republic. If allowed, this would be dangerous, as West Indian Negroes had been recently emancipated.[17]

One of the many difficulties facing Henderson and others of her representatives abroad was that of defective credentials. Everything was in short supply in the new Republic. Sam Houston used a cuff-link for a great-seal in the early days. There was little knowledge of diplomatic niceties as practiced in Europe, and the credentials were often very informal.

Then, too, other representatives were often sent to the same country on similar missions, thus confusing the foreign governments and casting doubt on the validity of the credentials of the first agent. Often the first was not informed of the mission of the second. Henderson worked under three chief executives; Burnet, Houston and Lamar, and this further confused the Europeans. They were used to the Cabinet system, where a change of government meant a change of policy. There were several Secretaries of State while Henderson was in Europe, and several changes of the capital city. These were some of the procedural difficulties facing the young Texas diplomat.

Knowing that he would need new credentials, since Lamar had succeeded Houston as President, he wrote to Irion, the Secretary of State, saying that the first credentials were "grossly informal," and giving specific instructions as to the preparation of new ones. The President was to be sure to sign his name at the bottom of the page. Evidently this had not been done before. Also, he insisted that the great seal be placed on the document with "wafors." He explained that these formalities were always necessary in Europe, with no exceptions for representatives of republics.[18]

Henderson had promised Molé he would wait for Saligny's report before making any further advances, and he really did wait for once, in spite of his persistent nature. However, he improved his time by enlisting the aid of Lewis Cass to speed-up negotiations with France. Cass was the Minister of the United States, which had already recognized Texas. Cass tried, but without success, but he interested the King of Belgium in Texas and was a great help in these negotiations.[19]

A letter to Memucan Hunt, now Secretary of the Texas Navy, in the spring of 1839, shows Henderson's interest in Texas affairs in spite of his European surroundings. He asked the news of Texas and especially about the French agent, Saligny, and stated that the King of France was favorable, though a change of ministry was expected. Henderson stated that he would like very much to be in the next Texas Congress, in the House, as he had many laws and amendments to propose for the welfare of Texas. He expected to be in the Republic before November, and would be a candidate from Harrisburg County (now Harris County), provided the "election was sure." His secretary, George McIntosh, wished to remain in France or England as his successor in case recognition was secured. Since Hunt was a fellow North Carolinian and an old friend, Henderson then became more personal, saying his time in France had been spent agreeably, and:

> My position enables me to obtain the entree to the best society. The consequence is that I have been compelled to spend much more money than is convenient from my private fortune.

He further stated that the Texas government would have to raise the pay of its Ministers to France and England, or no one but a man with a fortune could afford to accept the office. Little did he suspect that American diplomats would be voicing the same complaint one hundred years later. This letter closed with a reference to his health, which had suffered from the cold winters. He felt he must spend the next winter in the South.[20]

Now appeared on the scene a man who was to

cause Henderson a great deal of difficulty and embarrassment; General James Hamilton. He had had a colorful career in South Carolina in politics, and had great ability in business and finance.[21] His name was first connected with Henderson's in the Texas records in a letter Hamilton wrote to Lamar, who was then vice-president, in April of 1838. R. C. Saunders of Macon, Georgia, was introduced as having land scrip received as payment for the outfitting of Henderson for his trip to Europe.[22] Hamilton was busy then and later in various schemes of floating loans and selling bonds for Texas in the United States and European countries. He offered to go to Europe as a commissioner or agent, if given powers and discretion, as well as a liberal commission to hire agents.[23] Later he wrote that he wanted no public or official diplomatic appointment, but did request a letter to the Ministers of Foreign Affairs of England and France. He stated that he was a "friend of General Henderson" and expressed his "earnest concurrence with him." He wanted his agency to be secret and confidential, and expressed an intention of working with Stevenson in London and Cass in Paris (U.S. Ministers).[24]

Hamilton also had trouble getting proper credentials. In a letter to Lamar from Augusta, Georgia, in the spring of 1839, he told of five million dollars in bonds which he was to attempt to sell in Europe, but this would be dependent on France's recognition of Texas. He was leaving for Europe with Saligny on June 13, and again asked for a formal commission showing his association with Henderson, or at least a letter of authorization. A financial panic was on as the result of Biddle's resignation from the Bank of the United States, and it was a very difficult time to raise money.²⁵ Hamilton and Saligny were to cause Henderson many a headache before their paths parted.

In a letter to Lamar in April, Henderson advised a blockade of the Mexican coast to force England to recognize Texas. He believed that the British would do so to protect their valuable investments in that unhappy republic. As a personal note, he mentioned his poor health, and the fact that his private business had suffered greatly in the two years he had been abroad. He stated that he wished soon to return to Texas.²⁶

Henderson wrote to Lamar in September of his disappointment at the appointment of Hamilton and of his first intention to relinquish his post, but after an explanation by the General, he decided to remain. We find the first mention of Saligny and his genius for making trouble for Texas. Pontois had made the terms harder after a talk with Saligny, who told the French government that Hamilton had orders to give practically any terms desired for France in return for recognition. This was very disappointing and would probably result in the necessity for more concessions to France.²⁷ Evidently Hamilton was made aware of this and wrote to Lamar that Henderson had thought before the General's arrival that his mission showed a lack of confidence in Henderson's work, but was now satisfied on that score. He then paid many compliments to Henderson's ability and discretion, stating that a full treaty of commerce and alliance would soon be negotiated with France.²⁸

We find in Lamar's papers a letter from Hamilton to Lord Palmerston in September stating that he was a deputy to General Henderson as a diplomatic agent to ask for recognition from Great Britain. If independence were recognized, Henderson would be in London in a few days to negotiate a treaty of amity and commerce.[29] It is very doubtful if Henderson appreciated these activities of Hamilton in London.

Samuel Roberts sent a letter of warning to Lamar from Washington, D.C., at this time. He informed Lamar that Henderson had been greatly mortified that the Texas government had not notified him of Hamilton's association with him in diplomacy, but had received the information from Hamilton himself. It was Roberts' belief that Hamilton would cause more trouble than all of Lamar's enemies. He was very dubious about Hamilton's grandiose schemes for raising money in Europe. He warned that if Henderson resigned and returned to Texas, it would cause a great deal of political trouble for the Lamar administration. Roberts suggested that the Secretary of State correspond with the heads of legations and be sure that nothing was done without advising them. He stated that the pride of Anson Jones and Henderson had both been wounded. Henderson had very nearly completed a good treaty when that "busybody" Saligny came in to try to "knock it in the head."[30]

As early as June of 1839, Henderson had had an interview with Baron Pontois, French Minister to the United States, who was on leave in Paris. Pontois was of the opinion that Texas should be recognized as independent, and told the King that Texas should be so recognized in "common justice."[31]

Dining with Marshall Soult, the new Foreign Minister, on July 16, Henderson received the impression that recognition had now been decided on. Soult admitted that he had received Saligny's report, and we know that it was favorable, if only because the "little whipper-snapper" wanted to be France's Minister to Texas. Since Soult was too busy to negotiate, Henderson asked that he be allowed to do so with Pontois and this was agreed to.[32]

An important discussion with Pontois was held on July 18. Pontois noticed that Henderson's credentials were signed by Houston, who was no longer President. The Texan tried to explain that conditions were different in a Republic from those in a monarchy and that a new administration did not necessarily mean a change in policy. Soult was satisfied, but felt compelled to mention the matter to the Minister of Foreign Affairs. The two men discussed slavery as a possible source of friction, with Henderson stating that the Texas Constitution prohibited the slave trade, direct or indirect. Slaves could be brought in only through the United States and they must have been legal slaves in that country. Internal slavery was purely a domestic policy in Texas.[33]

Pontois expressed his opinion that France would make a commercial treaty and recognize Texas as independent in the same act. Henderson protested this, feeling that recognition should come first, so that the two countries could negotiate as equals on a commercial treaty. There was some discussion on tariff duties.[34]

Pontois began to ask for better terms on French imports into Texas, probably due to Saligny's influence. Henderson objected to a reduction of duties on brandies on both moral and financial grounds, but made some concessions. Nevertheless, Pontois withdrew his previous concessions on Texas cotton.

After Hamilton's arrival in Paris, the French emphasized the aid that recognition would give to selling Texas bonds. At first refusing tariff concessions, Henderson was persuaded by Hamilton to accept the terms offered rather than to write to the President for advice. The treaty was presented to the King on September 25, 1839.[35]

There were twenty articles and three "additional articles." The most important were as follows:

1. Citizens of each nation were to be guaranteed the rights and privileges of the most favored nation.
2. In case of war with a third power, neither was to issue letters of marque.
3. The flag was to cover the goods, and citizens of enemy or neutral vessels were not to be seized unless "actually engaged in the service of the enemy."
4. In case of war by one of the nations, the other was to have freedom of commerce with the exception of contraband of war, but not in case of an actual blockade.
5. Consular offices were to be established in the ports of each nation.
6. Tonnage duties in coastal waters were to be paid by ships of each nation as paid by vessels of the respective countries.
7. A duty of twenty francs per one hundred kilograms was to be charged on Texas cotton.
8. One-half duty was to be paid in Texas ports on French manufactured goods, mainly silks.

9. French wines were to enter Texas at two-fifths rate, and French brandies at one-fifth rate.
10. The treaty was to be ratified within eight months.

The three "additional articles" were to be secret, and were intended to conceal from other nations the fact that Texas had agreed to a different qualification of a Texas vessel than the one she had been insisting on; that is — only that her ownership be by a Texas citizen. The secrecy was to prevent other countries from demanding similar provisions.[36]

In a letter to Lamar, Henderson gives details of the official signing of the treaty. There was a speech by King Louis Phillipe, in which he praised Texas and its representative. He spoke especially of Henderson's courtesy and of the richness and the many advantages of Texas. Henderson then responded with a short speech, stressing the fact that France was the first nation of Europe to recognize the young republic.[37] The document was signed by Marshall Soult, by the King, and by James Pinckney Henderson.

The treaty with France was presented to the Texas Senate by Lamar on January 11, 1840.[38] A resolution was introduced on January 13 to ratify the "treaty of amity, commerce, and navigation."[39] The Senate gave its approval on January 14, and thus became officially operative the first European recognition of Texas.[40]

In his letter of September 26, Henderson had stated that he felt the treaty was not as favorable as it should have been or as just, but the best that could be made under the circumstances. He did not say so, but intimated that, without the interference by Hamilton and Saligny, he could have made a better agreement. He tells the President that Hamilton is leaving soon for Texas and will explain it to him. Henderson continues that in three days he will go to London for a conference with Lord Palmerston, and will then return to Paris in October to introduce General McIntosh to Marshall Soult as chargé d'affaires. There is again a reference to his health being impaired, which his physician has attributed to the severe winter climate.[41] Certainly, the long hours and persistent work on the treaty had done nothing to improve Henderson's health. He worked at diplomacy as hard as he had when studying law at Chapel Hill.

Hamilton, in a letter from New York to Lamar in October, praised Henderson's ability and fidelity and said that he (Henderson) wished to return to France as resident Minister.[42] Hamilton was evidently in error about this fact, as Henderson had no intention of spending another winter in Paris. In fact Lamar had other plans for the returning diplomat. In a message to the Senate on January 20, 1840, Lamar stated that Vice-President Burnet had been acting as Secretary of State due to a vacancy in that office. The President had planned to keep the office open and offer it to Henderson in case he did not want the office of Minister to France, but since Burnet refused to serve any longer, he submitted the name of Abner S. Lipscomb for the office of Secretary of State.[43]

What about the significance of Henderson's diplomacy in Europe? Sexton says this in his memorial address:

He acquired for Texas — then weak and maintaining a bare existence as a separate nationality — a position of respectability and dignity. Texas should ever be grateful for his services, and proud of her adopted son.[44]

Hampson Gary gives us these statements in a quotation whose author is not mentioned:

> His eminent talents and noble bearing, and the fidelity and zeal with which he urged the claims of his country to a place among the nations, engaged for him a warm personal consideration. His appeals for the recognition of that independence which Texas had so nobly achieved fell in stirring strains upon the proud ears of the great statesmen and diplomatists who at that time adorned the Courts of St. James (sic) and St. Cloud. It is said that in Paris he was looked upon as a new apparition of American glory, as another Franklin, fresh from the cradle of liberty.[45]

---

[1] J. W. Schmitz, *Texan Statecraft*, p. 64.

[2] Herbert Rook Edwards, "Diplomatic Relations Between France and the Republic of Texas, 1836-46," *Southwestern Historical Quarterly*, XX (1917-1918), pp. 209-241, pp. 341-357. This reference, p. 210. Hereinafter referred to as H. R. Edwards, "Diplomatic Relations with France." Also see J. W. Schmitz, *Texan Statecraft*, pp. 67-68. These difficulties are sometimes called the "Pastry War" because of the claim of a French baker for payment for pastries taken by some of Santa Anna's soldiers in 1833.

[3] Edwards, "Diplomatic Relations with France," p. 210. Also see J. W. Schmitz, *Texan Statecraft*, pp. 68-69.

[4] Henderson to Molé, May 26, 1838, from George P. Garrison, *Diplomatic Correspondence of the Republic of Texas*. Quoted in H. R. Edwards, "Diplomatic Relations with France," p. 209.

[5] *Ibid.*, p. 210.

[6] *Ibid.*, pp. 210-211.

[7] *Ibid.*, p. 211. Also, J. W. Schmitz, *Texan Statecraft*, p. 67.

[8] H. R. Edwards, "Diplomatic Relations with France," p. 211.

[9] *Ibid.*, p. 212.

[10] *Ibid.*, p. 212.

[11] *Ibid.*, p. 213. Also J. W. Schmitz, *Texan Statecraft*, p. 67.

12 Irion to Henderson, Sept. 7, 1838, quoted in H. R. Edwards, "Diplomatic Relations with France, p. 213.
13 Henderson to Irion, October 28, 1838, J. W. Schmitz, *Texan Statecraft*, p. 71. Also H. R. Edwards, "Diplomatic Relations with France," p. 213.
14 *Ibid.*, p. 214. Saligny was that mixture of French patriotism and pride, mixed with an eye to his own profit and advancement. After he was appointed chargé d'affaires to Texas in 1839, he received a national salute on arrival, passed counterfeit money to his teamster on arrival in Austin, and refused any redress. He was to be one of the main beneficiaries of the Franco-Texienne scheme to settle French settlers on the frontier in exchange for three million acres of land, which failed to pass the Texas Senate, though it passed the House. Saligny was the victim of the famous "pig incident." Texas journalists had a field day in commenting on this incident and on the land bill, thus greatly injuring the absurd dignity of the little Frenchman. His influence caused the failure of the badly needed loan from J. Lafitte and Company in 1841, as Humann, the French Minister of Finance, was his brother-in-law. Saligny shook the dust of Texas from his feet shortly afterward, but returned to Texas in April of 1844 at the invitation of Houston. He was called "a sort of mistletoe sprig of the French *noblesse*," by David G. Burnet. He left in Austin the French Embassy building which still stands. It is the only building ever built in Texas by a foreign government after its independence.
15 H. R. Edwards, "Diplomatic Relations with France," p. 214. Also see J. W. Schmitz, *Texan Statecraft*, p. 72.
16 H. R. Edwards, "Diplomatic Relations with France," pp. 215-216. Also J. W. Schmitz, *Texan Statecraft*, p. 72. (Henderson to Irion, November 12, 1838).
17 Henderson to Lamar, *Lamar's Papers*, II, pp. 290-291.
18 J. W. Schmitz, *Texan Statecraft*, p. 73.
19 *Ibid.*, p. 73.
20 Henderson to Hunt, March 29, 1839, *Lamar's Papers*, II, 508-509.
21 According to Adams, *British Interests in Texas*, footnote, p. 36, Hamilton was born in South Carolina in 1788 and was the son of a "favorite aid (sic) of Washington." He was educated for the law, was the Mayor of Charleston, a member of Congress (1822-1829). He was the "nullification governor" of South Carolina, though having been a strong Jackson supporter. He was a strong states' rights man and free trader. Disgusted with the nullification effort, he moved to Texas and was made a citizen by legislative act, was offered the command of the Army, refused, and it was given to Felix Huston. His efforts at raising financial aid for the empty Texas treasury were indefatigable in the United States and Europe, and his diplomatic efforts to secure recognition also were valuable. He had broad, sometimes visionary, ideas of empire for Texas, and was a strong opponent of annexation. He was drowned in a collision at sea, after giving up his seat in a lifeboat to a lady passenger.
22 Hamilton to Lamar, April 4, 1838, *Lamar's Papers*, II, p. 49.
23 Hamilton to Lamar, April 11, 1838, *Lamar's Papers*, II, p. 138.

24 Hamilton to Lamar, September 4, 1838, *Lamar's Papers*, II, p. 212.
25 Hamilton to Lamar, April 14, 1839, *Lamar's Papers*, II, pp. 526-527.
26 Henderson to Lamar, April 23, 1839, *Lamar's Papers*, II, p. 540.
27 Henderson to Lamar, September 1, 1839, *Lamar's Papers*, III, pp. 92-94. Also H. R. Edwards, "Diplomatic Relations with France," p. 222.
28 Hamilton to Lamar, Aug. 29, 1839, *Lamar's Papers*, III, pp. 82-84.
29 Hamilton to Palmerston, September 18, 1839, *Lamar's Papers*, III, pp. 111-112.
30 Samuel A. Roberts to Lamar, September 24, 1839, *Lamar's Papers*, III, pp. 115-117. Henderson had mentioned in one letter his anxiety at the internal dissensions in Texas. Houston and his friends were bitter political opponents of Lamar and critical of his extravagance, his Indian campaigns, and the expensive Army intended for Mexican conquests; especially when the Republic was so desperate for funds and its currency and credit so low in value.
31 Henderson to Burnet, Secretary of State, June 13, 1839; H. R. Edwards, "Diplomatic Relations with France," p. 219.
32 *Ibid.*, p. 220. Also J. W. Schmitz, *Texan Statecraft*, p. 76.
33 H. R. Edwards, "Diplomatic Relations with France," p. 221.
34 *Ibid.*, p. 222.
35 *Ibid.*, p. 223.
36 *Ibid.*, pp. 223-225. Also J. W. Schmitz, *Texan Statecraft*, pp. 78-79. This treaty is written in parallel columns in French and English. The original is in the State archives in Austin, Texas. It is bound in blue velvet sealed with the great seal of France, and attested to by Marshall Soult, the Duke of Dalmatia. Facsimiles of the first and last pages of the treaty are in Zachary F. Fulmore, *The History and Geography of Texas as Told in County Names* (Austin, Texas: The Steck Company, 1915), pp. 291-292.
37 Henderson to Lamar, Sept. 1839, *Lamar's Papers*, III, p. 118.
38 *Secret Journals of the Senate*, pp. 168-169.
39 *Ibid.*, p. 171.
40 J. W. Schmitz, *Texan Statecraft*, p. 79.
41 Henderson to Lamar, Sept. 26, 1839, *Lamar's Papers*, III, p. 118.
42 Hamilton to Lamar, Oct. 11, 1839, *Lamar's Papers*, III, p. 130.
43 *Secret Journals of the Senate*, pp. 173-174.
44 Sexton, "James Pinckney Henderson," pp. 190-191.
45 Hampson Gary, "General J. Pinckney Henderson," *Southwestern Historical Quarterly*, XLIX (Oct. 1945), p. 283.

Chapter 6

Marriage and Return to Texas

HENDERSON HAD NOT spent all his time in Paris on official business. He had also negotiated a personal alliance with Miss Frances Cox of Philadelphia. Miss Cox had been born in the Quaker City on July 21, 1830, and was thus nineteen years of age at the time of her marriage, Henderson being thirty-one. Her parents were John Cox of Philadelphia and Martha Lyman of Northampton, Massachusetts. Mr. Cox was in Paris to educate his two daughters and a son. At the time she met the Texan, Frances Cox had been studying in Europe for about ten years. She had great ability as a linguist, and was said to be able to read the Bible in French at the age of six, also excelling in mathematics and music.

Because of Miss Cox's devotion for the Church of England, the young couple crossed the channel to be married in St. George's Chapel in Hanover Square, London. The ceremony was performed in October of 1839. Shortly thereafter Henderson and his bride made preparations to sail for Texas, taking passage on an oceangoing steamer and arriving at Galveston in January of 1840.[1]

A great banquet and ball were given for General and Mrs. Henderson in Galveston to celebrate the great diplomatic accomplishments of the General and to welcome home the young couple.[2] Other banquets were planned in different parts of Texas, but Henderson refused them politely. He was too modest a man to enjoy these affairs in his honor, and he was anxious to establish his home in San Augustine and to begin again the practice of law.[3]

San Augustine must have been quite strange to Frances Henderson. Texas towns of the eighteen-forties were not noted for their culture and ease of living. The Hendersons lived in a log house at first, with a few slaves to help make a home.[4] However, San Augustine was far ahead of most of the Republic in civilization and culture, as this statement by Hogan shows:

> . . . in the early eighteen-forties San Augustine had been notable not only for two praiseworthy educational ventures, but also for the high cultural level of many of its citizens. Indeed, San Augustine of that day must provide a notable exception to any attempt to characterize the Republic of Texas as devoid

of the best in the civilization of the period. Even now, a century later, something of the atmosphere of good taste still lingers in the fine clear-cut lines of its old homes.[5]

The two "educational ventures" mentioned were San Augustine University, founded in 1842, and Wesleyan Male and Female College in 1844.[6]

Henderson soon built a fine new home which is described by Hogan as having "simplicity in general outline combined with neo-classic details of dignity and charm." This "two-and-one-half story residence, modeled after a well-known Virginia residence, has upper and lower galleries supported by large columns and is appropriately located in an oak grove." The general pattern was Greek Revival, showing a kinship with the plantation South. "On the whole, to the traveler of the eighteen-forties, San Augustine presented surprisingly few marks of frontier crudity."

Fire was a constant problem. In 1845, a fire in San Augustine destroyed several buildings before it could be checked by tearing down a building in its path. Thus we see that the town to which the gently reared Frances Cox came in 1840 was somewhat ahead of most of Texas in many respects. Mud, stumps and ditches ten or fifteen feet deep were great inconveniences and hazards in most Texas towns, especially at night. In Columbia, the capital, in the autumn of 1836, a man died after falling over a stump in the dark.[7]

There were many men and women in East Texas of education, culture and refinement. The Right Reverend Alexander Gregg, for thirty years Episcopal Bishop of the Diocese of Texas, who had been ordained in South Carolina, stated that he found many families in the San Augustine and Nacogdoches area that compared favorably to the people in his circle in South Carolina in "refinement, good breeding and social graces."[8]

San Augustine was one of the oldest settlements in Texas. It had been named for the Mission built by Franciscan Friars in 1717. The town itself was founded in 1832. At that time two squares miles of land sold for ninety dollars. The deed was dated January 26, 1833, and the 640 acres for the townsite sold for two hundred dollars. The first Protestant Church in Texas was built in San Augustine in 1839; the founder being Littleton Fowler, whose remains are today buried underneath the pulpit of a Methodist Church nine miles east of present day San Augustine. His monument serves as a rostrum.[9]

Mrs. Henderson was greatly interested in religious work, and there was certainly a great need for it in the Texas Republic. Scepticism was especially prevalent among doctors and lawyers, and many who had been religionists in their former homes found it difficult to maintain their piety in Texas. Fierce sectarian battles between various faiths, and within one denomination, turned many away from church affiliation. Non-observance of the Sabbath was general. About one-eighth of the white population of Texas were church members by the end of 1845, according to Hogan.[10] Frances Henderson worked faithfully in a Union Sunday School, composed of men and women of all beliefs, in which about seventy-five were enrolled. Young people were trained, and literary and musical entertainments were given. Mrs. Henderson was an accomplished performer on the piano and the harp.[11]

Several years after the Hendersons' arrival, an Episcopal Church was organized in San Augustine. Mrs. Henderson, according to Pickrell, gave seven thousand dollars from her private purse to construct the church building, also furnishing the altar with silver and linen, and providing a small reed organ. In addition, she trained a choir for the Episcopal service, which attracted many from great distances. Such pageantry, form, and glitter were extremely rare in pioneer Texas.[12]

James Pinckney Henderson was never a member of any church, though he was said to have a very religious nature. According to Sexton, when Henderson was on his deathbed, he confided to friends "that though he had made no ostentatious profession of religion, yet that he had felt it in his heart."[13]

Several Masonic lodges were established in Texas in the days of the Republic, and San Augustine had one of the first. Members from Houston, Nacogdoches, and San Augustine organized the Grand Lodge of Texas in 1837.[14] Sexton states that Henderson was a "devoted friend and patron of the Order." He joined late in life, for the reason that he would not associate with some of the shadier characters who were members in the early days. He was made a Master Mason in Red Land Lodge No. 3 in December of 1852, being greatly "impressed by the ritual," and "a zealous and faithful craftsman."[15]

Mrs. Henderson must certainly have been a busy woman in a religious way. Sarah McLendon says that, in addition to founding the church at San Augustine, she also established churches in Marshall, Nacogdoches, and Rusk, and is credited with establishing the episcopacy in East Texas.[16]

53

Henderson had returned to his adopted country at a poor time to take up again the practice of his profession. The late thirties had seen a great deal of prosperity, but the eighteen forties brought on a bad depression. Many felt that there were too few farmers and too many gentlemen who had come to Texas, not to labor, but to make their fortune in other ways.[17] The former diplomat wrote to one of his friends in 1840 that he was about to settle in San Augustine, since there was more law business there than in any other part of the Republic. He thought his practice there might be worth ten thousand dollars a year in "good money." How wrong he was is shown by the testimony of Thomas J. Rusk, Henderson's partner in one of the best law firms in the country. Rusk said in 1845 that the practice of law would scarcely support a man because of poverty in the nation, Mexican disturbances, and the large stock of young lawyers. It was necessary for lawyers to branch out into other fields: political jobs, plantation operation, and acquisition of land. The mediocre and the young lawyers taught school, preached, published newspapers, laid out new towns, kept hotels and boarding houses, and farmed. Some even became barbers. There were great problems involved in changing from Spanish law to the English Common Law. Henderson and his partners were, of course, far above these "cornstalk lawyers," as they were called, but their great numbers made remunerative practice more difficult.[18]

We find this statement in Hogan's *Texas Republic*:

> While many poorly educated lawyers were allowed to practice, the leadership of the Texas bar included some very talented individuals and a few with genuine

claims to distinction. Thomas J. Rusk of Nacogdoches and his partners, J. Pinckney Henderson and Kenneth L. Anderson of San Augustine, were very able and rendered signal service to the Republic.

Hogan states further that "the Temple Bar of the Young Republic at San Augustine probably had the highest level of legal talent in Texas."[19]

Much of the legal business in Texas was concerned with land claims. Many companies had been organized in the United States that had very shaky grants to Texas lands, or none at all. Even the most eminent lawyers found themselves involved in attempts to validate claims for which thousands of dollars of worthless scrip had been sold. Henderson, Sam Houston, and John C. Watrous were employed by the Galveston Bay and Texas Land Company, one of the largest and most notorious of these land promotions, but they failed to validate most of the claims. Houston made speeches denouncing the "unholy dictation of speculators and marauders upon human rights," but his private dealings were different.[20] Most lawyers of Texas at that time had many such cases, and most engaged freely in land speculation themselves. The sad recent experience of the United States with Western lands had made little impression in Texas.

There are many testimonies to the legal ability and distinction of J. Pinckney Henderson. Note this statement by Norman Kittrell:

> Governor Henderson would have risen to distinction in any state because he was endowed by nature with the elements of leadership. The late Governor Roberts knew him intimately and well. They lived in the same section of Texas and practiced in the same courts

55

... Governor Roberts was a competent judge of ability in men, and I heard him say on one occasion that J. Pinckney Henderson was the ablest man ever in public life in Texas.

Also:

He was a man of very wonderful oratorical ability, and had the power of fascinating audiences and thrilling them with his eloquence; and in that day and time a man who possessed that power, coupled with even a moderate amount of legal ability, was destined to succeed in a new country like East Texas was at that time, and the success of General Henderson was conspicious because he was both eloquent and able.[21]

Sexton, who lived in San Augustine for many years and knew Henderson intimately, testifies to his eminence at the bar and some of the reasons for his success. He states: "Not many lawyers can boast of a more successful professional career (than that) of General Henderson. I doubt if many have even equalled his success." He practiced over the entire country, where difficult and important cases were to be tried. He had great fidelity to his clients, by no means a common trait among lawyers at that time. The controlling traits of his character were sincerity and ingenuousness, says Sexton, and this was especially outstanding in his professional life. In his treatment of a witness he would never try to trap or browbeat him, but he was merciless if one evaded or contradicted himself. Never indulging in equivocation or deceit, opposing counsel were never afraid of his taking a technical advantage. The young lawyers loved him because he was always ready to assist and instruct and because of his kind manner to them at all times. So says F. B. Sexton.[22]

There were exceptions, of course. Some young lawyers were very vain, ignorant and boastful; and even insulting to the judge. One of these was William C. Duffield, indicted for forgery connected with election returns, and also defendant in a suit brought by Sam Houston to remove him from the practice of law. This was in the term of 1840-41 of the District Court of San Augustine, and Henderson was prosecuting the forgery case. Duffield became angry and made some insulting remarks about Henderson, was reproved by the Court, and thereupon insulted the Judge, George W. Terrell. Judge Terrell fined the young lawyer five hundred dollars for contempt of court. Duffield then replied, "You may say a thousand dollars." The judge obliged, and also sent him to jail.[23]

As F. B. Sexton had so many opportunities to observe Henderson at work in his legal practice, it is probably worthwhile to look at more of his observations. He states:

> As a lawyer, he was distinguished for the vigor of his mind, the clearness and quickness of his perceptions and the perspicuity of his reasoning.

His early training had been thorough and accurate, and he had given careful attention to elementary and general principles. "Probably no man understood better than he the great fundamental principles of the common law."

Henderson regretted that his large and laborious practice permitted little legal reading. His legal opinions were from reasoning from elementary principles rather than from judicial precedents, and yet his opinions were almost invariably concurred in by the higher courts. Henderson was gifted with an extraordinary memory. There were no written digests of opinions in the courts where he practiced, and yet he could take a certain principle and tell all about it, before whom an applicable case was tried, how it arose, and the full extent and limitation of the decision.[24]

Since Henderson had so little time for legal reading, and since competent law clerks were even scarcer than able lawyers, Mrs. Henderson took up the study of law herself, and from all reports became very proficient at it, though she never took a bar examination or practiced. She did much of the office work for Henderson and handled duties in the office when he and his partners, Anderson and Rusk, were away on business. In view of her brilliant intellect, we may surmise that she was well able to master the precepts of the law.[25]

There were the usual joys and sorrows for the Hendersons. Five children were born to them, the first two failing to survive their infancy, but three daughters lived to brighten the home of the busy attorney. Their names were Frances, Julia, and Martha.[26]

As a resident of San Augustine, his neighbors rated the eminent attorney a very public-spirited man; one whose funds and influence could be counted on to back any public improvement. He was noted for his help to the poor and other unfortunates. His legal services were always available without charge to those in need of them and unable to pay a fee. Henderson's courtroom plea for a fatherless boy indicted for assault on a man who had insulted his mother brought many in the courtroom to tears.[27]

His sense of honor and his unswerving regard for the truth were well known throughout Texas. Lynch tells of an incident in France that illustrates his love for veracity under all conditions. While negotiating with the French diplomats for recognition for Texas, so important to the new Republic, Henderson was asked to give the population of Texas. There were no accurate census figures at the time, but he was ashamed to say what he thought it was, even in the field of diplomacy, where deceit was more or less expected. As a way out, he asked a French nobleman present, who was a friend of Texas and had recently paid a visit to the country, what his estimate was. The reply was "about a million." The diplomats were amazed at the figure, but did not question it, though it was really about fifty thousand.[28]

Shortly after his return to Texas in 1840, Henderson was urged to run for President, as Lamar's term was soon to end. His reply was that the Constitution required a man of at least thirty-five years of age, and he was several years short of that. His friends then urged that he run anyway, stating that he was generally taken for forty, and that no one would know the difference. His reply was promptly that he would ". . . never violate the Constitution of my country, though no one on earth would know it except myself." "My own heart," he said, "would know it, and would condemn me."[29]

Thus for several years, the man who, at the age of thirty-one, had already been a brigadier-general, attorney general, secretary of state, envoy and minister to Europe, and one of the Republic's most eminent attorneys, was able to turn to his private affairs,

59

establish a home, and enjoy a respite from the tension of public affairs. Soon, however, he was to be called by the march of events to the public arena once more, and to give freely of his time and talents to the beloved land of his adoption.

---

1 Annie Doom Pickrell, "Mrs. J. Pinckney Henderson, Born Frances Cox," *Pioneer Women in Texas* (Austin, Texas: The Steck Company, 1929), pp. 172-179. This reference, pp. 172-173. Hereinafter referred to as: Pickrell, "Mrs. J. Pinckney Henderson."

2 De Shields, *High Place,* p. 168, footnote.

3 Sexton, "J. Pinckney Henderson," pp. 191-192.

4 Pickrell, "Mrs. J. Pinckney Henderson," p. 173.

5 Hogan, *Texas Republic,* p. 153.

6 *Ibid.,* pp. 152-153.

7 *Ibid.,* pp. 29-30. Henderson's home still stands in San Augustine, in good condition, but it was remodeled in 1936, and its top story removed.

8 Norman G. Kittrell, *Governors Who Have Been and Other Public Men of Texas* (Houston, Texas: Dealy-Adey-Elgin Company, 1921), p. 14. Hereinafter referred to as Kittrell, *Governors Who Have Been.*

9 Fred I. Massengill, *Texas Towns* (Terrell, Texas: Publisher not shown, 1936), p. 162.

10 Hogan, *Texas Republic,* pp. 191-194.

11 Pickrell, "Mrs. J. Pinckney Henderson," pp. 172-173.

12 *Ibid.,* pp. 175-176.

13 Sexton, "J. Pinckney Henderson," p. 202.

14 Hogan, *Texas Republic,* p. 217.

15 Sexton, "J. Pinckney Henderson," pp. 200-201.

16 Sarah McLendon, "Tyler D.A.R. Seeks Return of Sword from Germany," Houston *Chronicle,* (September 16, 1945), p. 8B. Hereinafter referred to as McLendon, "Return of Sword."

17 Hogan, *Texas Republic,* p. 17.

18 *Ibid.,* p. 247.

19 *Ibid.,* p. 252.

20 *Ibid.,* pp. 82-83.

21 Kittrell, *Governors Who Have Been,* pp. 13-14.

22 Sexton, "J. Pinckney Henderson," p. 193.

23 Hogan, *Texas Republic,* pp. 257-258. Other difficulties of the courts were: fears of personal violence, Indian and Mexican raids (as that of General Woll on San Antonio and his capture of the district court in session), and the tolerance toward murder. Legal action against a murderer in northeast Texas was possible only if the motive was robbery or

the murder was in cold blood.
[24] Sexton, "J. Pinckney Henderson," pp. 192-193.
[25] Pickrell, "Mrs. J. Pinckney Henderson," p. 173. Also McLendon, "Return of Sword."
[26] Pickrell, "Mrs. J. Pinckney Henderson," p. 176.
[27] Sexton, "J. Pinckney Henderson," p. 201.
[28] Lynch, *Bench and Bar of Texas,* pp. 192-193.
[29] Sexton, "J. Pinckney Henderson," pp. 191-192.

Chapter 7
Election As First Governor of the Lone Star State

EVENTS WERE MOVING rapidly to place Texas even more in the forefront of the national and international scene. The quiet though busy life of an attorney in East Texas was about to come to an end. The years of 1844 and 1845 were to be momentous ones in Texas and in the life of James Pinckney Henderson, one of its most eminent citizens.

To review very briefly the annexation question is appropriate, but no detailed discussion will be attempted here.

Texas was a republic from March 2, 1836, to December 29, 1845. One of the main issues voted on in the first national election was whether or not Texas should become a member of the Union. Only ninety-one out of almost six thousand votes were cast against it. It was thought at the time that there would be little difficulty, and that the United States would be delighted to secure this huge addition to its territory. However, Memucan Hunt, the Texas agent in Washington, found that such was not the case. Secretary of State Forsythe delayed action, saying that treaty obligations with Mexico prevented consideration of the proposal.

Annexation was discussed in Congress in 1838, but no action was taken, and, as we have seen, Texas withdrew its offer on January 23, 1839. The matter was not reopened until 1843.

Isaac Van Zandt, the Texas chargé d'affaires at Washington, was negotiating for annexation in 1843-44. President Sam Houston sent Texas' most famed diplomat, J. Pinckney Henderson, as Minister-plenipotentiary to assist Van Zandt. A treaty was successfully negotiated with Upshur and Calhoun, successive United States secretaries of state, and signed by Calhoun, and the Texas representatives on April 12, 1844, but the treaty was rejected by the United States Senate.[1]

After the election of Polk in November on the main issue of the "re-annexation" of Texas and "reoccupation of Oregon," President Tyler placed the matter again before Congress, urging this time a joint resolution instead of a treaty. Such a resolution needed only a majority vote of each house. On February 28, 1845, the resolution was carried by a vote of 27-25 in the Senate and 120-98 in the House.[2]

The last Congress of the Republic was called into

extraordinary session by President Anson Jones at Washington-on-the-Brazos on June 16. It promptly accepted the offer of annexation, and called a convention to draw up a constitution for the new state which was to be submitted to the voters along with the question of annexation.

This convention, says Sexton, is generally thought to be the ablest political body ever assembled in Texas. Henderson was one of its leading members, being a delegate from San Augustine County. One example of his participation, of which we have a record, is that in the debate over exclusion of ministers of the gospel from the legislature. This clause was in the constitution of the Republic, and was proposed for inclusion in the new state constitution. Henderson spoke against the proposal, saying he did not think it appropriate for ministers to engage in political contests, but thought that the matter should be left for their own consciences. He thought that such a clause was a reproach to the ministry and would deprive a citizen of one of the basic rights of free men. His motion, when made, was seconded by Thomas J. Rusk, but even the influence of these two great public men was not sufficient. The clause was placed in the new constitution.[3]

Lynch tells us that Henderson was one of the most active and influential members of the convention, and that many of his views were adopted.[4] The delegate soon to be first governor of the new state was a member of the committee on education. This body had seven members, three of the others being Edward Clark, Judge R. E. B. Baylor, and E. H. Tarrant. Among the recommendations made to the convention by this committee was the following:

> The Legislature shall, as early as practicable, establish free public schools throughout the State, and shall furnish means for their support by taxation on property, and from and after the year eighteen hundred and fifty, it shall be the duty of the Legislature to set apart one-tenth of the annual revenue of the State, as a perpetual fund, the interest of which, at six percent per annum, shall be apportioned to the support of the free public schools; and no law shall ever be made, directing said funds to any other use.[5]

When this was presented to the convention, an amendment was offered from the floor to strike out *shall* and substitute *may*. This was strongly opposed by the committee and was rejected by a vote of thirty-seven to eleven, Henderson being one of those voting against the change. The educational provision was somewhat modified before being added to the constitution, but the mandatory provision requiring the setting aside of one-tenth of the annual revenue of the state for a perpetual fund was retained.[6]

The proposed state constitution was ratified by the voters on October 13, 1845, who at the same time voted overwhelmingly to join the Union. The constitution was accepted by the United States Congress and President Polk late in December. This is the language of that resolution:

> Be it resolved by the Senate and House of Representatives of the United States of America in Congress assembled, That the State of Texas shall be one, and is hereby declared to be one, of the United States of America, and admitted into the Union on an equal footing with the original States, in all respects whatever.[7]

The Henderson family had a tradition of interest in government and politics, and James Pinckney was no exception. As a leading attorney of the new state, and having held many appointive positions under the Republic, it was only natural that he should consider public office a duty and an interesting pursuit. We have seen that, while still in Europe, he expressed a possible desire to run for office as a member of Congress from Harrisburg County. In a letter to Memucan Hunt, he indicated that he would like to run for the House, provided "election was sure"; and also stated that he had many laws and amendments to propose.[8]

Sexton appraises Henderson as a Jeffersonian Democrat, supposedly meaning one who favored states' rights. He was said to be active in politics but very scrupulous not to advocate anything or support any principle in which he did not believe. "He was one of the few public men who acted on the maxim of Paley that 'What is morally wrong cannot be politically right'."[9]

It may be difficult to understand how a man as cultured and well-educated as Henderson, and a man of such high moral character, as well as modesty and self-effacement, could be a popular political figure in a time of such rampant individualism and violence as Texas in the time of the Republic. But Henderson was also a man of great courage, who more than managed to stand up for his rights and to maintain the respect of all classes. Otherwise, he could never have been elected governor and have managed to command the tough Texas volunteers in the Mexican War.

Duels were frequent among the leading men of

the Republic, the most famous perhaps being that in which Albert Sidney Johnston was severely wounded by Felix Huston. Memucan Hunt challenged Lamar in 1842, because of the latter's charges that Hunt had attempted to have Henderson recalled from France, so that Hunt could secure his appointment for himself. A group of men, headed by General Johnston, mediated and prevented the encounter.[10]

Fights were even more frequent than duels, and men of all classes participated in them. The floors of Congress were not immune to these affrays. Some men were participants through no fault of their own, as the fights were forced on them. Some of these were such celebrated Texans as John S. Ford, William Barrett Travis, Judge John M. Hansford, Alexander Horton, and Kenneth L. Anderson, the law partner of Henderson.[11] If a public man was challenged and refused to fight, he was branded as a coward and that was fatal to his future career. There were gunmen and bullies who made a career of swaggering about looking for encounters. Such a man ran afoul of J. Pinckney Henderson, to his sorrow, and that of his survivors.

This encounter is best told in a letter written by Henderson to Ashbel Smith, his personal friend:

> I had been annoyed for more than a year by a desperado named N. B. Garner, whom I was at last forced to Slay a few weeks since. He had often threatened to kill me and twice when I was unarmed he attempted to assassinate me. I had a abhorrance to the shedding of human blood in a street fight and laboured to avoid it as it never in my estimation adds to a man's reputation — A few days before I killed Garner he waylaid me with a double-barreled gun to assassinate me as I passed but I learned his movements

and avoided him — from that time I marked him as my own. He was preparing to shoot me when I shot him and was closely watching an opportunity to take some advantage of me for he was a coward and would not attack me with pistols when I was similarly armed or on the look-out. I regret that the beast forced me to do that which some ruffian ought to have done but I shall never regret that I killed him as I am sure he then would have killed me if I had not slain him . . . I demanded an investigation of the affair after I killed Garner and the court of inquiry declared me fully justified.[12]

Kittrell states that any man that could not rise fearlessly to such a situation in that day and time could not hope to have an active career at the bar in East Texas. The typical "bad man was present then on the border of civilization as he has always been, and it was the misfortune of a gentleman to be compelled to rid the community of one of that class, though he did thereby render a public service."[13] There is no doubt that J. Pinckney Henderson had the respect of the citizens of Texas and could hold his own in any situation.

Candidates had appeared early for the offices of the new state, even during the campaign for annexation. The two chief candidates for governor were Kenneth L. Anderson and Dr. James B. Miller. Anderson was the vice-president under Anson Jones and was still presiding over the Senate in the Ninth Congress in June of 1845. He was a native of Lincolnton, North Carolina, the home town of Henderson, having come to Texas in 1837. Associating with Rusk and Henderson in the most famous law firm in Texas, Anderson was usually considered the most eloquent of the three. He was conceded to be the most likely candidate to become the first governor under the flag of the Union. However, on his return home from the last session of the Congress, he became suddenly ill and died on July 3, 1845 at the old town of Fanthorpe, later named Anderson in his honor. Henderson was then prevailed on to become a candidate and thus fell heir to the support previously given to Anderson, as well as having the advantage of his own great popularity. In the first general election held for state office, on the third Monday in December of 1845, Henderson received 7,853 votes out of a total of 9,578 cast. Albert C. Horton was elected Lieutenant Governor.[14]

The First Legislature of Texas met on Monday, February 16, 1846, for organization. General Edward Burleson, the old Indian fighter, was elected President Pro Tempore of the Senate, and W. E. Crump of Austin County was chosen Speaker of the House. The only business was the appointment of joint committees to wait on the governor-elect and inform him of his election. Henderson reported that his choice for inauguration day was Thursday, February 19. Rev. William Morrell was elected chaplain of the House, but the eccentric Senator Robert M. Williamson (Three-Legged Willie), prevented the election of a chaplain for the Senate.[15]

On the appointed inauguration day, at Austin, on February 19, the seats were removed from the House and Senate chambers and placed on the long gallery on the east side of the capitol. Members of the Legislature were seated here and hundreds of citizens gathered before the appointed hour. "There was little conversation — a hush seemingly induced by an effort to stifle emotion difficult to master. Many gazed with evident affection at the Lone Star Flag. . . ."[16]

The Capitol was decorated with flags, both of the Lone Star and the Stars and Stripes. The retiring President and the governor-elect appeared; escorted by a joint committee of both Houses, as well as military officers of the United States, who had already been stationed at the Texas capital.[17]

To begin the ceremonies, the invocation was delivered by Judge R. E. B. Baylor, former Kentucky legislator, member of the Alabama legislature, Congressman from Alabama, soldier in the Creek Indian War, Texas district judge, minister, and co-founder of Baylor University. His prayer was said to have the "rich fervor of the Christian patriot."[18]

Anson Jones then delivered his valedictory address. It was universally applauded for its good taste and appropriate sentiment. Here are some interesting excerpts:

> The great measure of annexation, so earnestly discussed, is happily consummated. The present occasion, so full of interest to us and to all the people of this country, is an earnest of that consummation; and I am happy to greet you, their chosen representatives and to tender you my cordial congratulations on an event the most extraordinary in the annals of the world; one which marks a bright triumph in the history of republican institutions. A government is changed both in its officers and in its organization — not by violence and disorder, but by the deliberate and free consent of its citizens; and amid perfect and universal peace and tranquility, the sovereignty of the nation is surrendered and incorporated with that of another.[19]

The close of President Jones' address often quoted:

> The Lone Star of Texas, which ten years ago arose amid clouds over fields of carnage obscurely seen for awhile, has culminated, and following an inscrutable destiny, has passed on and become fixed forever in that glorious constellation which all freemen and lovers of freedom in the world must reverence and adore — the American Union. Blending its rays with its sister States, long may it continue to shine, and may generous heaven smile upon the consummation of the wishes of the two republics now joined in one. May the Union be perpetual, and may it be the means of conferring benefits and blessings upon the people of all the States, is my ardent prayer. The final act in the great drama is now performed. The Republic of Texas is no more![20]

The President's remarks, according to contemporary newspaper accounts were interrupted with frequent bursts of applause, which were promptly suppressed, as it was felt that this type of demonstration ill-suited the solemnity of the occasion.[21]

As the last sentence was uttered by President Anson Jones, the Lone Star flag of Texas was lowered and the boom of artillery sounded to commemorate the fact. Almost immediately the Stars and Stripes were raised to the top of the standard. All were glad to see it there, and yet many old pioneers felt strong emotions as they recalled the years of struggle and danger and the love they had had for the Republic. It was a very impressive scene.[22]

The oath of office was then administered to the governor-elect by W. E. Crump, the Speaker of the House. Then James Pinckney Henderson, nearing his thirty-eighth birthday, delivered his inaugural address, one of the shortest on record. Some pertinent sections are as follows:

> Gentlemen of the Senate and the House of Representatives: This day and within this hour has been consummated the great work of annexation. This consummation, it seems to me, should be a full compensation to our citizens for all their toils and sufferings endured for ten long years. Our hearts should be full of gratitude to the Giver of all good, for the many favors He has bestowed at all times and under all circumstances. . . . He is still with us. Who can look back upon our history and not be fully and deeply impressed with the consideration that the arm of Deity has shielded our nation, and His justice and wisdom guided us in our path? It is therefore our duty, in deep humility, to make our acknowledgements for His many favors. . . . It is with a deep sense of responsibility which I have incurred, that I now enter upon the duties of the station which my fellow citizens have called me to fill.
> . . . Let us then, I beseech you, commence our existence as a State of this great Union, in the spirit of harmony and forbearance, and act our parts throughout as becomes the agents of a free enlightened, Christian people.
> . . . We have this day fully entered the Union of the North American States. Let us give our friends, who so boldly and nobly advocated our cause, no reason to regret their efforts in our behalf. Henceforth, the prosperity of our sister states will be our prosperity — their happiness, our happiness — their quarrels, our quarrels, and in their wars we will freely participate.[23]

Congratulations were received from old Andrew Jackson, almost at the end of his life; who appreciated the value of the addition of Texas to the Union, and congratulated the United States as well.

Jackson always thought of the act as the "re-annexation of Texas." He said:

> I now behold the great American eagle, with her stars and stripes, hovering over the lone star of Texas, with cheering voice welcoming it into our glorious Union, and proclaiming to Mexico and all foreign governments, "You must not attempt to tread upon Texas — that the United Stars and Stripes now defend her."[24]

Col. John S. Ford summed things up in his *Texas Democrat*:

> Texas is secure in the enjoyment of all that a patriot could wish — her destiny is united to that of the mightiest people on earth. Her watchword must be "Union" and her progress will be "Onward."[25]

---

[1] Lynch, *Bench and Bar of Texas*, p. 188. Also De Shields, *High Place*, p. 168. Many Texans were disappointed at this additional snub to the offer of annexation, but Texas was fortunate that it was not accepted. Terms of the annexation in 1845 were much more favorable, as the state was to keep her public lands, while under the 1844 agreement these lands were to go to the national domain of the Federal government. Thus, an immensely valuable resource was retained.

[2] The date of final passage of the joint resolution is given by some sources as March 1, instead of February 28. The full text is found in John Henry Brown, *History of Texas* (St. Louis: L. E. Daniell, 1892), II, pp. 306-307.

[3] Sexton, "J. Pinckney Henderson," pp. 194-195.

[4] Lynch, *Bench and Bar*, p. 188.

[5] Joseph W. Hale, "Masonry in the Early Days of Texas," *Southwestern Historical Quarterly*, XLIX, pp. 380-381.

[6] *Ibid.*, pp. 380-381.

[7] From *Telegraph and Texas Register*, Houston, January 14, 1846. Llerena Friend, Ed., "Contemporary Newspaper Accounts of the Annexation of Texas," *Southwestern Historical Quarterly*, XLIX, p. 268. Hereinafter referred to as, Friend, "Contemporary Accounts."

[8] Henderson to Hunt, March 29, 1839. *Lamar's Papers*, II, p. 508.

[9] Sexton, "J. Pinckney Henderson," pp. 197-198.

[10] Hogan, *Texas Republic*, p. 285.

11 *Ibid.*, p. 271.

12 November 25, 1842, Ashbel Smith papers. Quoted in Hogan, *Texas Republic*, p. 274. Hogan states that many entries in the minutes of the San Augustine County District Court show that Henderson's estimate of Garner was correct.

13 Kittrell, *Governors Who Have Been*, p. 14.

14 De Shields, *High Place*, p. 169. The vote for lieutenant governor was a very close affair. Horton won over Nicholas H. Darnell by a majority of 120 votes. The legislature, in joint session, first declared Darnell elected, but after returns from a missing county arrived, Horton was declared the winner. Brown, *History of Texas* (footnote), pp. 308-309. Some newspaper accounts at the time gave Henderson 8,190 votes to Miller's 1,672. From New Orleans *Times-Picayune* issue of March 3, 1846. Correspondence from "Paul," dated February 18, 1846 from Austin. Friend, "Contemporary Accounts," p. 275.

15 Friend, "Contemporary Accounts," pp. 273-275.

16 Excerpt from report in *Texas Democrat*, by Editor John Salmon Ford in *Under Texas Skies*, I, No. 10 (March, 1951), p. 46.

17 De Shields, *High Place*, pp. 169-170.

18 *Ibid.*, p. 170.

19 Brown, *History of Texas*, II, pp. 309-310.

20 Francis Richard Lubbock, *Six Decades in Texas* (Austin, Texas: Ben C. Jones and Company, 1900), p. 179. Jones' address may also be found in full in "Contemporary Accounts," pp. 275-278.

21 Friend, "Contemporary Accounts," p. 275.

22 *Under Texas Skies*, I, No. 10, p. 47.

23 *Ibid.*, pp. 48-49. Also in Brown, *History of Texas*, II, p. 310 and in Friend, "Contemporary Accounts," pp. 278-279.

24 Brown, *History of Texas*, II, p. 310.

25 Lubbock, *Six Decades in Texas*, p. 179.

Chapter 8

Chief Executive and Major General of Texas Volunteers

AS IN ALL the other public positions Henderson had held, the problems he faced as Governor of Texas were staggering. The public debt was very large, in spite of the preceding economical administrations of Sam Houston and Anson Jones. Mexico was threatening invasion over annexation. Texas borders were uncertain on every side except the Gulf of Mexico, and the Indians on the frontier were still a great problem. There were procedural details of the changeover from a republic to a state which were complicated and arduous. State revenues were a greater problem than they had been under the Republic, since the tariff, its main source of revenue, could no longer be collected; though there was no longer the expense of diplomatic representation or regular armed forces.

Appointments made by the new governor included the following: Secretary of State, David G. Burnet; Attorney General, John W. Harris; Comptroller, James B. Shaw; Treasurer, James H. Raymond; Commissioner of the General Land Office, Thomas W. Ward; Adjutant-General, William G. Cooke. All of these had had experience under the Republic. The Supreme Court of the State was composed of John Hemphill, Chief Justice, and Abner Lipscomb and Royal F. Wheeler, Associate Justices.[1]

Sam Houston and Thomas J. Rusk were elected by the Legislature as United States Senators from Texas.

In his first message to the Legislature, Governor Henderson spoke of three things that were very close to his heart — economy in government, improvement of the court system, and the establishment of a public school system. Concerning the state's need for schools, he said:

> The prosperity, happiness, and permanence of every government like ours, where all authority is derived from and exists at the will of the people, greatly depends upon the intelligence and moral and religious character of its citizens. The prosperity, happiness and permanence can be best secured to ourselves and posterity by making liberal provisions for the education of the rising and future generations. By the constitution it is made the duty of the Legislature to make suitable provision for the support of public schools,

and to set apart not less than one-tenth of the annual revenue of the State as a perpetual fund for that purpose, and as soon as practicable to furnish other means for the support of the free schools throughout the State by taxation. The slow progress made by most of our sister States in collecting a sufficient fund for educational purposes and maturing plans for public schools, should warn us of the necessity of commencing that important work with our earliest existence as a State.[2]

The governor recommended in his message the immediate revision of civil and criminal law — "A faithful and rigid administration of the criminal laws of every State is necessary; the public peace, safety, and morals demand it."[3]

As to economy, the message contained the following statement:

> Economy in the administration of the government is always becoming to the agents of the people — with us it is absolutely necessary.[4]

The concluding statement of the message:

> I commend to you, gentlemen to God's holy care, with a full reliance upon His bountiful providence for the prosperity of our infant State. As He has conducted us through all our dangers and troubles to the desired haven, so will He enable us to ride there in safety. He will keep us in the right path and point out the way in which we may perpetuate our free government.[5]

Texas, however, was not yet to be free to develop the arts of peace. Mexico had given warning that annexation would be considered an act of war, and moved up troops to the Rio Grande. In response to this, United States troops under Gen. Zachary Taylor moved to the border. Fighting began on Texas soil on April 25, 1846, General Taylor immediately calling on Texas for troops. In a short while four regiments of infantry and cavalry and two regiments of Texas Rangers were raised and equipped. The famous Jack Hays and Col. G. T. Wood were the commanders of the Rangers. De Shields says that altogether about eight thousand volunteers from Texas served in the Mexican War.[6]

The Legislature of Texas, on May 9, 1846, passed the following resolution:

> Resolved, That James Pinckney Henderson, Governor of the State have leave and authority, under this resolution to take command in person of all troops raised (in this State) and mustered into service by order of the general government, according to the constitution and laws of the United States.
>
> Approved May 9, 1846.[7]

Henderson was given a commission by the United States as Major General in command of Texas Volunteers. On his staff were Ex-President Lamar, Gen. Edward Burleson, Henry L. Kinney, and Edward Clark, later to be governor of Texas. Lamar was later stationed at Laredo with an independent force, with Hamilton P. Bee as his second in command.[8]

To his bitter disappointment, at the time of the departure of the Texas troops for Mexico, Henderson was ill in bed. His arduous duties as chief executive of the new state had weakened his never robust constitution, and he was forced to allow the troops to leave without their commanding officer. However, in one week, this letter was received by Lieutenant Governor Horton:

Executive Department
Austin, May 19, 1846

To His Excellency
A. C. Horton

Sir,

I shall this day leave the seat of the government to take command of the Texas forces raised under the requisition of General Taylor and shall move beyond the Rio Grande into Mexico. Under these circumstances, you are required by the Constitution to act as governor of the state of virtue of your office of lieuenant-governor.

I have the honor to be,

Your obedient servant
(Signed) J. Pinckney Henderson[9]

After writing this letter, he left in a carriage without escort of any kind. This was a dangerous business, as he was driving through hostile country, with bodies of Mexican troops moving about, but the trip was made successfully and he joined the United States forces on the road to Monterrey.[10]

General Henderson caught up to the main force on the afternoon of September 18, arriving with the two regiments of Texas Rangers under Colonels Hays and Wood.[11] These forces were to become famous for their marksmanship and bravery, and McCulloch's company of Ranger Scouts established themselves as the equal of any scouting force in the history of warfare.

This was the order of battle on the march to Monterrey: Captain Gillespie's Ranger Company, McCulloch's Rangers and the rest of the regiment, Col. Jack Hays, Col. G. T. Woods' Texas Rangers (under the direct command of Henderson), the First Division under General Twiggs, the Second Division under General Worth; with the Third Division in command of General Butler bringing up the rear. Here is a vivid picture of the march as seen by one of McCulloch's Rangers:

> Advancing in solid battalions and moving, as it were, like the ocean's swell, with the sun's rays glittering upon the arms of the dark and serried ranks, and the bright artillery flashing in the midst, they formed a noble and imposing pageantry.[12]

Monterrey was strongly fortified, and was naturally protected by surrounding mountains and hills. Its defenders outnumbered the invaders considerably, and the Americans had only a few light pieces of artillery instead of heavy siege cannon generally considered necessary for reduction of a strong fortress. Added to these difficulties was a lack of provisions, tents, and overcoats for the men; greatly needed during the current rainy season with chill winds blowing out of the mountains.

Gen. Zachary Taylor, "Old Rough and Ready," was not a very good general as far as strategy and tactics were concerned, but most of the rank and file loved him; he had great courage and soldiers would follow him anywhere. He was said to have one eye on the Presidency as he fought his battles; and this may have been so, but the fact remains that he won his battles. His efforts were sometimes greatly handicapped by large numbers of his men leaving for home when their enlistment periods were up, many having volunteered for only three months' service, and others for only six.

When these handicaps are considered, however, we must list several great advantages. The regular army officers, Worth and Twiggs, were sound strategists and tacticians. The marksmanship of the Americans was greatly superior to that of the Mexicans, and their courage in battle was fabulous. Finally, the Texas Rangers formed a superb force that could fight equally well mounted or on foot, and McCulloch's Scouts became the indispensable eyes and ears of the Army. The Texans and most of the other volunteers were a great problem when not fighting, but in battle they were a problem only to the enemy. General Taylor is reported to have said that Texans were neither cowards nor gentlemen.

Nearing the city, The Second Dragoons and Colonel Woods' "Texian" Rangers under command of General Henderson were ordered to proceed toward the northern limits of the city to make a demonstration at the upper part, and to support General Worth if it became necessary.[14]

A body of Mexican lancers was reported to be moving on the plain. Henderson with Woods' Rangers went in pursuit, but no hostile forces were encountered after a search of five or six miles.[15]

The three-day battle for Monterrey began with the capture by the Americans of the two fortified hills on the west of the city, on one of which was the Obispado or "Bishop's Palace." Henderson played no part in this, as he was on the other side of town. At the end of the first day the fighting stopped because in the darkness no one could tell friend from foe. General Worth ordered all positions held except those of the Texans under Hays on the side of town fronting on the Santa Catarina River. Their horses needed attention, and the men were needed for pickets and other rear duties.[16]

Early fighting around the edges of the city had caused few American casualties, largely because of the poor marksmanship of the Mexican forces, but the street fighting was a different story. Raw courage and persistent advance in the face of death were the things that carried the day for the Americans. The eyewitness account of one of McCulloch's Rangers can scarcely be improved upon for vividness and stark reality. A small part of his account follows:

> Every street was barricaded with heavy works of masonry, the walls being some three or four feet thick, with embreasures for one or more guns which raked the streets; the walls of gardens and sides of houses were loop-holed for musketry; the tops of the houses were covered with troops, who were sheltered behind parapets some four feet high upon which were piled sand bags for their better protection, and from which they showered down a hurricane of balls.[17]

And another passage:

> The street-fight became appalling — both columns were now close engaged with the enemy, and steadily advanced inch by inch — our artillery was heard rumbling over the paved streets, galloping here and there, as the emergency required, and pouring forth a blazing fire of grape and ball — volley after volley of musketry, and the continued peals of artillery became almost deafening — the artillery of both sides raked the streets, the balls striking the houses with a terrible

crash, while amid the roar of battle were heard the battering instruments used by the Texians. Doors were forced open, walls were battered down — entrances made through the longitudinal walls, and the enemy driven from room to room, and from house to house, followed by the shrieks of women, and the sharp crack of the Texian rifles.[18]

Many famous names are found on the roll of those who battled through the shell-torn streets of Monterrey on the final day of its siege; Braxton Bragg, Jefferson Davis, General Worth, and Zachary Taylor himself. Along with them was Gen. James Pinckney Henderson of the Texas Volunteers.[19]

Samuel Reid gives us a few eyewitness views of Henderson's part in this sanguinary fighting. The Texas general had been out scouting with Wood and on returning, "dismounted, entered the city, and forcing his way under a heavy fire of musketry and grape, soon came up with the advance." General Lamar joined the Texans and fought his way from house to house, approaching to within about a block of the Cathedral plaza. The general with the heroic name had become a private to get a chance to fight Mexicans at San Jacinto, and he was now getting in his second licks. General Taylor at this point ordered a retirement to the captured forts to plan a concerted attack on the city.[20]

In this third day of the battle, as Henderson led the Second Texas Regiment in person, he was cut off while reconnoitering and narrowly escaped capture or death by crawling back on his hands and knees.[21] Col. Jefferson Davis of the Mississippi Rifles gives us a good picture of the situation:

85

On the third and last day of the attack, when the night was closing around us, and we were near to the main plaza, we learned that we were isolated; that orders had been sent to us to retire; that the supports had been withdrawn, and that we were surrounded by a large number of the enemy. A heart less resolved, a mind less self-reliant than Henderson's might have doubted, wavered and been lost. The alternative was presented to him of maintaining a post which he was confident we could hold or of retiring, when it was doubtful whether we could cut our way through the enemy; he asked no other question than, "Are we ordered to retire!" On learning that such was the fact, he decided, at whatever hazard, to obey; and in that occasion escaped with his life.

The sense of duty rose with him superior to all other considerations; and he obeyed an order which he might have been justified in disobeying, because of the dangers to which it would subject him.

He was as gentle as a lamb in the hour of peace and in the midst of friends; but bold as the lion in the face of danger and when confronted by an enemy.[22]

Vivid pictures of the battles in and around Monterrey are found in letters to Henderson in the form of reports on the actions that took place. One of these was from Col. G. T. Wood, later to become the second governor of Texas, and dated September 24. Colonel Wood commanded the Second Regiment of Texas Mounted Volunteers.[23] The other report was made by the famous Col. Jack Hays, Commander of the First Regiment of Texas Mounted Volunteers.[24] Of course, General Henderson knew about these events, but reports were necessary to get them on the record.

On the morning of September 24, a bugler from the Mexican positions sounded a parley. Shortly thereafter a Mexican officer, Colonel Moreno, rode out toward the American lines with a white flag. He was accompanied by several other officers, and bore a letter from Gen. Pedro de Ampudia, the commanding officer of the Mexican forces, to General Taylor. A meeting was arranged for one o'clock to discuss the terms of capitulation, and commissioners were chosen from each side. For the Mexicans the commissioners were Generals J. Manuel Ortega and P. Requena and Don Manuel M. Lleano, governor of Nuevo Leon. The United States forces were represented by Brig. Gen. William J. Worth of the United States Regular Army, Col. Jefferson Davis of the Mississippi Rifles, and Maj. Gen. J. Pinckney Henderson, commander of Texas Volunteers. After quite a bit of discussion, the terms were agreed to and signed late in the day, though the actual, final surrender did not take place until the next day. The terms seemed generous — too generous to most of the Texans.[25]

Ampudia was allowed to retire from Monterrey with all his troops and their small arms, and in addition, one small battery. American forces agreed not to advance for a period of eight weeks beyond a line formed by the Pass of the Rinconada, the city of Linares and San Fernando de Pasos.[26]

General Taylor, in his report to the United States government, gave his reasons for the lenient terms as, the gallant defense of the city, and a recent change of government in Mexico which he believed favorable to peace, and which he wished to encourage. There were undoubtedly other reasons; among which were the lack of heavy artillery in the United States forces, shortage of ammunition, and shortage of most other supplies; including forage for horses, food for the troops, and coats and blankets as protection against the cold, rainy weather.[27] Many military students have since agreed that the Mexican forces could not have been prevented from evacuating the city if they had desired to, though they would have had some losses. American forces were too small to have prevented a withdrawal.

Though an enormous amount of military stores and supplies fell to the invading forces by the capitulation, the Texans were not appeased. Many were maddened with disappointment that the Mexican forces had been let off so easily, but they gradually calmed down.[28] There was no such revolt against discipline as took place over the disposal of Santa Anna after San Jacinto. Henderson later said he was opposed to the leniency of the terms, but was acting under orders.

What had caused General Ampudia to surrender; with ample supplies and in possession of strongly fortified positions, and a force superior in numbers? Many Mexican officers said the answer was his cowardice, but there were other things as well. Many influential city and state officials had put pressure on him to surrender to avoid further destruction of the city. American artillerymen had got hold of a mortar and had begun to drop shells in the main plaza of the city. An explosion in front of the Cathedral had done a great deal of damage and killed several people. Since the ancient Cathedral was crammed with munitions of all kinds, a shell that would set them off could cause immense destruction to the main part of the city. This is said to be the chief reason for Ampudia's capitulation.[29]

On September 25 the ceremony of surrender took place. The Mexican flag came down from the citadel and the Stars and Stripes were hoisted in its place.[30] A few days later, on September 30, the Texans were mustered out of service and the two regiments disbanded, though other companies were raised and served in later campaigns.[31]

Henderson returned to Texas and resumed the governorship on December 13, 1846, having been on military service seven months, lacking six days.[32] He had refused to accept his pay as governor, and received only his salary as major general during the seven months he was serving in Mexico.[33] It was remarkable that a man of his frail constitution, recently risen from a sickbed, could have endured the rigors of a military campaign and the strenuous effort of fierce combat, but evidently his spirit triumphed over his infirmities.

A great public dinner was given in Austin in honor of the governor and major general shortly after his return from the campaign. Attending were men of all varieties of political beliefs. Many toasts were delivered, with appropriate "airs," as was the custom of that time. Some of the "regular" toasts were: "The President of the United States" air, "Hail Columbia"; "The Subjugation of Monterrey, may those who achieved it reap the reward of their valor" air, "Yankee Doodle"; "The Army and Navy of the United States — the Army has drawn the sword with cause, it will not sheathe it without honor, the Navy, it bides its time"; "The Volunteers of Texas — let those who died at Monterrey be remembered with the martyrs of the Alamo, let those who survive be enrolled with the victors of Bexar and San Jacinto, the subjugation of the former gave us confidence, the triumph of the latter established our independence";

"General J. Pinckney Henderson, our distinguished guest — the victorious chief warm in the hearts of his countrymen, not only for his prowess in the field, but for his distinguished talents as a statesman." A short response was made by Henderson; due to his ill health, he did not say much more than that he had opposed the liberal terms given to General Ampudia, and had signed only on the orders of General Taylor. He also paid high tribute to the bravery of the Texas Volunteers. The gathering was then treated to a recitation of Potter's "Hymn of the Alamo," and Ira Munson's "Our Flag." The evening closed with a ball.[34]

Further honors were to come from the United States government, which voted him its official thanks and a gold-hilted sword for his services in the Monterrey campaign.[35]

In the remainder of Henderson's term as governor, he was busy with further organizing and stabilizing the state government. There were problems of protecting the frontiers against Mexicans and Indians, and disputes with the United States over the borders of Texas. It has been mentioned that Lamar had been given command of a force at Laredo to control the uneasy frontier. In a letter to Henderson on March 3, 1847, he said the Mexicans and Indians in that vicinity were dangerous, and that he needed at least three hundred troops, as the enlistments of many were expiring. He asked for permission for a leave of absence to enlist reinforcements. Lamar wrote a letter in similar vein to Zachary Taylor at Buena Vista, and also asked for a more active command.[36] Garrison duty was not to Lamar's liking, as it was not to that of his troops. He had a great deal of trouble with discipline.

Writing to Lamar at Laredo in July, Henderson expressed displeasure at the fact that the Frontier Battalion under Col. Jack Hays had been ordered by General Taylor to report to him at Monterrey. Hays was then at San Antonio preparing to leave; against the wishes of most of his men. The Governor stated that he would call on the President for other forces to guard the frontier to be put under command of Lamar. He also sent word of Indian depredations at Corpus Christi, San Patricio, Goliad, and Davis' Bluff. Taylor gave an order on September 28, 1847 to raise a company with twelve months' enlistments to be stationed at Laredo.[37]

The occupation of New Mexico by United States troops early in the Mexican War brought on more headaches for the Governor of Texas. Brig. Gen. Stephen Kearney, in command of United States forces, had made a bloodless conquest and issued a proclamation from Bent's Fort on July 31, 1846. Kearney had secret instructions from Secretary of War William L. Marcy to set up temporary civil governments in both New Mexico and California as soon as the territory came under Military control, and to continue in office all officials that would swear allegiance to the United States. In a proclamation of August 22, General Kearney asserted that New Mexico was now a part of the United States, and would be called the Territory of New Mexico. The General then appointed himself governor in the absence of Governor Armijo. One month later Kearney issued an *Organic Law of the Territory of New Mexico,* appointed many territorial officers, and provided for the election of a territorial delegate to Congress. This was in violation of the Ordinance of 1787, which provided that Congress was to set up new territories and the President appoint officials with the approval of Congress. In this case Congress objected, and the Secretary of War told Kearney that he had no power to grant political rights under the Constitution, but that the United States had the right to set up a civil government in any conquered territory. He was ordered to maintain his government, but not to treat the territory as annexed to the United States. After much discussion in Congress, a resolution was passed to leave the question of the ownership of New Mexico until a peace treaty was signed with Mexico.[38]

In a letter to United States Secretary of State James Buchanan, Governor Henderson asked information about the accuracy of accounts in the newspapers about the claims of the "general government" to territory within the limits of Texas under the boundary act of December 19, 1836. He protested against any United States action interfering with the rights of Texas, but:

> Inasmuch as it is not convenient for the State at this time to exercise jurisdiction over Santa Fe, I presume no objection will be made on the part of the government of the State of Texas to the establishment of a territorial government over that country by the United States, provided it is done with the express admission on their part that the State of Texas is entitled to the soil and jurisdiction over the same, and may exercise her right whenever she regards it as expedient.[39]

President Polk replied that the military government in New Mexico was only one set up over conquered territory under international law for the purposes of preserving order and protecting the rights of the inhabitants. He further stated that this occupation would end with the treaty of peace and this temporary government would not affect the right of Texas to all of the territory east of the Rio Grande. The President concluded that the whole question was a matter for Congress to settle, rather than for the Chief Executive. This message quieted things down in Texas, but they were to boil up later on.[40]

The settlement of this boundary question was to be left to other administrations, but Henderson, as Texas' shrewdest diplomat, knew that it was vital to get one's position on the record and to get some commitment from the other side; both of which things he did. He thus paved the way for the final settlement, by means of which Texas disposed of all her indebtedness, and received the sum of almost four million dollars. Two million dollars of this amount was set aside in 1854 for public free schools. For a few years after this settlement, no taxes were levied or collected by the state. As James T. De Shields says, "Happy memory."[41]

Henderson had stated several times that he had no intention of running for a second term as governor. In a letter to Lamar at Laredo in August of 1847, he again stated this determination, saying his private affairs needed attention. He then discussed the candidates for governor, whom he named as "Van Zandt, Darnell, Wood, Robison (of Sabine), and Miller." He expressed the belief that either Miller or Van Zandt could win but he feared, if both ran, they "will weaken each other and Wood may in that way slip in. He is a great *dog*."[42] We hear nothing of Robison in the campaign, but the others were in the race. Isaac Van Zandt was favored, but died at Houston of yellow fever, and that allowed Wood to win the governorship by a vote of 7,154 to Miller's 5,106, with Darnell trailing with 1,276. Col. George T. Wood, whose report to Henderson after the Battle of Monterrey has been mentioned, was the brave and popular colonel in command of the regiment of East Texas Rangers. We have seen in Henderson's letter to Lamar that he was not a political favorite of the Governor. For some reason, Henderson failed to mention Wood's services at the battle in his report on the engagement, and this slight was used by his supporters as campaign ammunition. It no doubt aided in his election. John A. Greer was elected lieutenant governor.[43]

On December 21, 1847, Governor Henderson, after a busy, important, and dangerous two years, turned the governor's office over to Colonel Wood. The retiring governor, at the age of thirty-nine, had seen enough history in the making, taken part in enough public business, and lived through enough excitement for a dozen lives the length of his. He had aided at the birth and recognition of the Republic, and had smoothed the path of the new state and helped protect it from its enemies. James Pinckney Henderson, having literally worn himself out in the service of Texas for more than ten years, and made deep inroads into his private funds, had earned retirement to the private life that he desired and the practice of law that he loved.

At the time of the governor's retirement, the state was prosperous, and its development was promising. The census showed a population of 136,000, exclusive of Indians. Educational institutions were being established and trade was thriving. All in all, Henderson had a right to be content as he traveled to his home in East Texas.[44]

---

[1] De Shields, *High Place*, p. 171.
[2] Lynch, *Bench and Bar*, p. 189.
[3] *Ibid.*, pp. 189-190.
[4] *Ibid.*, p. 190.
[5] *Ibid.*, p. 190.
[6] De Shields, *High Place*, pp. 172-173. John Henry Brown puts the number at 8,018. *History of Texas*, II; p. 323.
[7] Brown, *History of Texas*, II, pp. 318-319.
[8] *Ibid.*, pp. 322-323.
[9] From Executive Record Book, Texas State Library, Austin, quoted in *Southwestern Historical Quarterly*, XLIX, p. 444.
[10] Lynch, *Bench and Bar*, p. 190. At this time Monterrey was almost universally spelled "Monterey," at least by Anglo-Saxons. Also, Matamoros was spelled "Matamoras."
[11] Samuel C. Reid, Jr., *The Scouting Expeditions of McCulloch's Texas Rangers*, (Austin, Texas: The Steck Company, 1935), pp. 140-141. A facsimile of that published in Philadelphia by G. B. Zieber and Co., 1847. Hereinafter referred to as Reid, *McCulloch's Rangers*.
[12] *Ibid.*, p. 141.
[13] Hogan, *Texas Republic*, p. 277.
[14] Reid, *McCulloch's Rangers*, p. 160.
[15] *Ibid.*, p. 189.
[16] *Ibid.*, p. 194.
[17] *Ibid.*, p. 192.
[18] *Ibid.*, p. 192.
[19] De Shields, *High Place*, pp. 172-173.
[20] Reid, *McCulloch's Rangers*, p. 197.
[21] Lynch, *Bench and Bar*, pp. 190-191.
[22] *Ibid.*, pp. 190-191.
[23] Wood to Henderson, September 24, 1846. *Lamar's Papers*, IV, Part I, pp. 136-138.
[24] Hays to Henderson, September 24 (?), 1846. *Ibid.*, pp. 138-140.
[25] Reid, *McCulloch's Rangers*, pp. 201-210. Also Brown, *History of Texas*, II, p. 333.
[26] Reid, *McCulloch's Rangers*, p. 210.
[27] *Ibid.*, pp. 201-202.
[28] *Ibid.*, p. 204. Also Brown, *History of Texas*, II, p. 333.
[29] Reid, *McCulloch's Rangers*, p. 205.
[30] *Ibid.*, p. 211.

31 *Ibid.*, p. 225.

32 Letter from Mrs. John Lee Smith to Weaver Baker, September 28, 1945, *Southwestern Historical Quarterly*, XLIX (1945-1946), pp. 446-447.

33 Sexton, "J. Pinckney Henderson," p. 197.

34 Lubbock, *Six Decades in Texas*, pp. 187-188.

35 The history of this sword is interesting. It was bequeathed by Henderson to the eldest son of his eldest daughter and was to be handed down continuously. His eldest daughter, Frances, while traveling with her mother in Europe, met and married Baron Clemens von Preuschen, a young officer in the Army of the Duke of Nassau, who later became a major general of the Austrian army. The Baron was a relative of the Duke of Nassau. The oldest son, Ernst, of the Baron and Frances Henderson was a captain in the Austrian Navy and later an officer of the guard of honor for the Emperor Franz Joseph. The sword has been in the possession of the Preuschen family at Parsh-Salzburg. The Tyler chapter of the Daughters of the American Revolution corresponded with the Family in 1939, and they expressed a wish to give it to Texas, but the war intervened. Efforts were made to have General Eisenhower, Marshall Stalin, and the State Department to facilitate the search for the sword in 1945, but as far as it is known there has been no success. Sarah McLendon, "Tyler D.A.R. Seeks Return of Sword from Germany," *Houston Chronicle*, (September 16, 1945), p. 8B.

36 Lamar to Henderson, March 3, 1847. *Lamar's Papers*, IV, Part I, pp. 161-162. Lamar to Taylor, March 1 (?), 1847. *Ibid.*, pp. 159-160.

37 Henderson to Lamar, July 14, 1847, *Ibid.*, pp. 174-175.

38 William Campbell Binkley, *The Expansionist Movement in Texas 1836-1850* (Berkeley, California: The University of California Press, 1925), pp. 141-148. Hereinafter referred to as Binkley, *Expansionist Movement*.

39 Henderson to Buchanan, January 4, 1847, in Senate Executive Documents, 31 Cong. First Session (Ser. 354) No. 24, p. 2. Quoted in Binkley, *Expansionist Movement*, p. 148.

40 *Ibid.*, p. 148.

41 De Shields, *High Place*, p. 160.

42 Henderson to Lamar, *Lamar's Papers*, IV, Part I, pp. 176-77.

43 De Shields, *High Place*, pp. 179-180.

44 *Ibid.*, p. 174.

Chapter 9

Closing Events of a Great Career

FOR TEN YEARS following his term as governor, Henderson led a quiet life as a private citizen. Rusk, one of his old law partners, was in the United States Senate, and Anderson, the other, was dead, but he acquired new partners and continued to practice law. As before, he was a strong supporter and worker for all good causes in his community and the state. His talent was available without charge for those without means to afford legal counsel. His health was failing and he gradually became more and more averse to mental or physical effort.[1] In 1856 Henderson moved his family to Marshall, which was to be his final home.[2]

In 1857, Thomas J. Rusk, the first United States Senator from Texas, committed suicide. To the vacancy thus created, the seventh Texas Legislature meeting at Austin in November, elected J. Pinckney Henderson as Senator to succeed his old friend and law partner, who had so tragically taken his own life. The election was almost unanimous for Henderson, his only opponent, G. S. Smyth, receiving only three votes.[3]

Almost at the end of his strength, the new Senator made the long and tiresome journey to the national capital. Shortly after assuming his duties, Henderson yielded to the grim reaper. His death occurred on June 4, 1858, in Washington, D.C., at the age of fifty. The man who served his state and nation practically all his adult life, and gave freely of his strength and his means came finally to the end of his short but productive life.[4]

According to the biographical directory of Congress, the duration of Henderson's service as senator is shown as extending from November 9, 1857 to June 4, 1858.[5] He is shown there as a resident of Marshville (sic) and as having taken his seat on March 1.[6]

The state funeral of the great Texan was held in the Senate chamber of the Capitol. Participating were the Senate and House members, the President of the United States and his Cabinet, the Diplomatic Corps, members of the United States Supreme Court, ranking officers of the United States Army and Navy, and his many grieving friends. Eulogies were delivered by Sam Houston of Texas, Jefferson Davis of Mississippi, John J. Crittenden of Kentucky, David S. Reid of North Carolina, Arthur P. Hayne of South Carolina, and William H. Seward of New York.[7]

In the House of Representatives, eulogies were given by Guy M. Bryan of Texas and John A. Quitman of Mississippi. The members of the Committee of Arrangements for the funeral as appointed by the Senate were: James A. Bayard of Delaware, Simon Cameron of Pennsylvania, Benjamin F. Wade of Ohio, James H. Hammond of South Carolina, and William H. Seward of New York.[8]

Pallbearers, chosen from the membership of the Senate, were: Albert G. Brown of Mississippi, James F. Simmons of Rhode Island, Thomas L. Clingman of North Carolina, Lyman Trumbull of Illinois, Graham N. Fitch of Indiana, and Henry Wilson of Massachusetts.[9]

Among the many tributes paid to the deceased senator, that of Seward of New York was outstanding. Here is a small part of his address:

> If anything on this occasion has seemed to me more worthy of remark than another, it is, that although Senator Henderson was yet a young man, he had been a most successful and fortunate man, and, at the same time, a type of the public man of America. In listening to the eulogisms which have been pronounced for him, I have been surprised as they have followed him from the bar to the head of a brigade, from the head of a brigade into the cabinet of his State, from the cabinet into a foreign mission, from the foreign mission back to the bar, from the bar, flushed with success, transferred again to the diplomatic corps — the ambassador of his State to form a union with the United States — thence back again to the bar, then a member of the Constitutional Convention to frame the organic law for his State, then the

Governor of that new but already great State, then a major-general in the Federal service, and, finally a Senator in the Congress of the United States. It is a singular and a successful career for a revolutionary man, a man who has spent his whole life in revolutionary times. It was his felicity, one which rarely happens to revolutionary men, that he did not survive either the fortune of his State or its favor.[10]

Sam Houston, Henderson's colleague in the Senate, paid him this tribute:

> James Pinckney Henderson was no ordinary man. He made his mark upon the history of Texas, and the nation is not unacquainted with his reputation. He will be long remembered. He was a bold, enterprising spirit; a man of indomitable will, of daring enterprise, and firm purpose. His intellect was of a high order and cultivated to the extent that opportunities of professional engagements would permit. This is the colleague whose loss I deplore, for the bereavement falls upon me as it will upon others. His friends had confidence in and were ardently attached to him; they were deeply devoted to him and the chord that is broken will be one of thrilling sensibility.[11]

Following the ceremonies in the Senate Chamber, the body of this great son of North Carolina and Texas was laid to rest in the Congressional Cemetery at Washington, D.C., but in April, 1930, his remains were removed to the Texas State Cemetery at Austin. Here, with suitable ceremonies, he was reinterred and a suitable monument erected over his grave.[12] The inscription on the stone recites his great services to the Lone Star State:

James Pinckney Henderson
Born at Lincolnton, N.C., March 31, 1808.

Brigadier-General in the Texas Army, 1836.
Attorney General. Secretary of State, 1836.
Special Agent from Texas to England and France, 1837.
First Governor of Texas, 1846-1847.
Major-General in the U.S. Army in charge of Texas Forces in the Mexican War, 1846-1847.
United States Senator, 1857.
Died at Washington, D.C., June 4, 1857. (sic) [13]

Erected by the State of Texas.

---

[1] De Shields, *High Place*, p. 174.

[2] "Wife of First Texas Governor, Mrs. James P. Henderson Was Woman of Unusual Ability," Dallas *Morning News* (January 14, 1940). Hereinafter referred to as "Wife of Texas Governor," Dallas *News*.

[3] Lubbock, *Six Decades in Texas*, p. 224.

[4] De Shields, *High Place*, p. 175.

[5] *Biographical Directory of the American Congress, 1774-1927.* (Washington, D. C.: United States Government Printing Office, 1928), p. 1086.

[6] *Ibid.*, p. 256. Mathias Ward of Jefferson was appointed to the seat vacated by Henderson and was seated December 6, 1858.

[7] Hampson Gary, "General J. Pinckney Henderson," *Southwestern Historical Quarterly*, XLIX (1945-1946), pp. 282-285. This reference, p. 284.

[8] *Ibid.*, p. 284.

[9] *Ibid.*, p. 285.

[10] *Ibid.*, p. 285.

[11] A. Henderson, "Two Tar Heels."

[12] De Shields, *High Place*, p. 175.

[13] This date should be 1858.

Chapter 10

Family Notes

PERHAPS A FEW WORDS should be said about the family that survived Governor Henderson, in addition to the facts already mentioned. Frances Cox Henderson perhaps deserves more attention than has been given to her. In personal appearance she was slender, had heavy dark brown hair, a fine complexion, and hazel eyes. Her great linguistic ability has been alluded to. French was the language of the Cox family, and all correspondence between her and her sister was in that language.[1]

Mrs. Henderson's maternal grandfather was Gen. William Lyman of Northampton, Massachusetts, an officer of the Connecticut forces in the Revolutionary War. John Cox, her father, was a merchant of Philadelphia, being president of the Lehigh Coal and Navigation Company, the pioneer in anthracite mining in Pennsylvania. Her one brother was James S. Cox, and her sister, Julia, married a Biddle of Philadelphia.[2]

As previously mentioned, Frances married Von Preuschen, and lived in Austria and Germany. Martha Lyman Henderson died unmarried, at the age of eighteen, in Schwalbach, Germany. Her body was laid to rest in a memorial chapel erected by her mother. The other daughter, Julia Biddle Henderson, married Edward White Adams of Louisiana on October 18, 1868.[3] They had met in Europe.

Julia must have been an interesting and venturesome soul, as this incident of her youth in East Texas shows:

> Miss Julia Henderson, daughter of J. Pinckney Henderson, introduced the novelty of swimming to the fair sex of the town. Miss Henderson rode daily to Ayish Bayou, on a mule, and went in swimming. Incidentally, Miss Henderson was a charming girl from all acounts, and was widely traveled and versant with at least four foreign languages.[4]

Mrs. Henderson, after her sojourn in Europe for several years following her husband's death, returned to Louisiana to visit her daughter, Mrs. Julia Adams. There she took a great interest in the slaves that had been freed by the Thirteenth Amendment. She wrote a sketch, "Prissel Baker, Freed Woman," and translated it into seventeen languages.[5]

Julia's husband, Edward Adams, after some residence in Europe, moved to East Orange, New Jersey, and became a broker in New York. Mrs. Henderson made her home with Julia and Mr. Adams in East Orange for the remainder of her life. While there she founded a home for aged women and also a welfare society. Without any previous illness, the wife of the first Texas governor died suddenly on January 25, 1897, at the age of seventy-seven.[6]

[1] "Wife of Texas Governor," Dallas *News*.
[2] *Ibid.*
[3] *Ibid.*
[4] Frank Thomas, "Tequitina! Cradle of Texas." Feature article in Houston *Post*, July 1, 1934.
[5] Pickrell, "Mrs. J. Pinckney Henderson," p. 178. Julia had one son, Pinckney Henderson Adams. Her only daughter was Julia, who married Arthur H. Geisler of Oklahoma City. Mr. Geisler became American Minister to Guatemala during the Coolidge administration. Mrs. Geisler passed away on February 14, 1925, and was buried in Oklahoma City in March of that year.
[6] "Wife of Texas Governor," Dallas *News*.

Bibliography

Adams, Ephraim Douglass. *British Interests and Activities in Texas, 1838-1846.* Baltimore: The Johns Hopkins Press, 1910.

Binkley, William Campbell. *The Expansionist Movement in Texas, 1836-1850.* Berkeley, California: The University of California Press, 1925.

Biographical Directory of the American Congress, 1774-1927. Washington, D.C.: United States Government Printing Office, 1928.

Brown, John Henry. *History of Texas.* St. Louis: L. E. Daniell, 1892, II.

De Shields, James T. *They Sat in High Place.* San Antonio, Texas: The Naylor Company, 1940.

Edwards, Herbert Rook. "Diplomatic Relations Between France and the Republic of Texas, 1836-1846," *Southwestern Historical Quarterly,* XX (1917-1918), pp. 209-241, pp. 341-357.

Friend, Llerena, Ed. "Contemporary Newspaper

Accounts, of the Annexation of Texas," *Southwestern Historical Quarterly*, XLIX (1945-1946), pp. 267-281.

Fulmore, Zachary Taylor. *The History and Geography of Texas as Told in County Names.* Austin, Texas: The Steck Company, 1915.

Gary, Hampson. "General J. Pinckney Henderson," *Southwestern Historical Quarterly*, XLIX (1945-1946), pp. 282-285.

Hale, Joseph W. "Masonry in the Early Days of Texas," *Southwestern Historical Quarterly*, XLIX (1945-1946), pp. 374-383.

Henderson, Archibald. "The Transylvania Company: A Study in Personnel. I. James Hogg." Pamphlet reprinted from *Tilson Club Historical Quarterly*, XXI. No. 1 (January, 1947), Louisville, Kentucky, pp. 1-21.

Henderson, Archibald. "The Transylvania Company: A Study in Personnel. II. Thomas Hart." Pamphlet reprinted from *Tilson Club Historical Quarterly*, (July, 1947), Louisville, Kentucky, pp. 228-242.

Henderson, Archibald. "Two Tar Heels Played Leading Role in Wedding Texas to American Union," Greensboro *Daily News* (April 22, 1928) Page not shown.

Henderson, J. Pinckney. "Inaugural Address," *Southwestern Historical Quarterly*, XLIX (October, 1945), pp. 278-279.

Hobbs, Samuel Huntington, Jr. *North Carolina, Economic and Social.* Chapel Hill, N.C.: The University of North Carolina Press, 1930.

Hogan, William Ransom. *The Texas Republic.* Norman, Oklahoma: The University of Oklahoma Press, 1946.

Horton, Lucy Henderson. *The Horton Family*. Franklin, Tennessee: Publisher not known, 1922.

James, Marquis, *The Raven*. New York City: Blue Ribbon Books, Inc., 1929.

Jones, Anson. *Memoranda and Official Correspondence Relating to the Republic of Texas, its History and Annexation*. New York: D. Appleton and Co., 1859.

Kittrell, Norman G. *Governors Who Have Been and Other Men of Texas*. Houston, Texas: Dealy-Adey-Elgin Company, 1921.

Lamar, Mirabeau Buonaparte. *Papers*. Austin, Texas: The Texas State Library, 1920. Edited by Charles Adams Gulick, Jr., and Katherine Elliott.

Lubbock, Francis Richard. *Six Decades in Texas*. Austin, Texas: Ben C. Jones and Company, 1900.

Lynch, James. *Bench and Bar of Texas*. St. Louis: Nixon Jones Publishing Company, 1885.

McLendon, Sarah. "Tyler D.A.R. Seeks Return of Sword from Germany," Houston *Chronicle* (September 16, 1945), p. 8B.

Massengill, Fred I. *Texas Towns*. Terrell, Texas: Publisher not shown, 1936.

Pickrell, Annie Doom. "Mrs. J. Pinckney Henderson, Born Frances Cox," *Pioneer Women in Texas*. Austin, Texas: The E. L. Steck Company, 1929, pp. 172-179.

Ray, Worth S. "Information on J. Pinckney Henderson," *Southwestern Historical Quarterly*, XLIX (1945-1946), p. 301.

Reid, Samuel C., Jr. *The Scouting Expeditions of McCulloch's Texas Rangers.* Austin, Texas: The Steck Company, 1935. A facsimile reproduction of the original published in Philadelphia: G. B. Zieber and Co., 1847.

Schmitz, Joseph William. *Texan Statecraft, 1836-1845.* San Antonio, Texas: The Naylor Company, 1941.

Secret Journals of the Senate, Republic of Texas, 1836-1845. Austin, Texas: Austin Printing Co., 1911.

"Selected List of References Relating to James Pinckney Henderson, (March 31, 1808-June 7 1858)." *Southwestern Historical Quarterly,* L. (1946-1947), pp. 147-151.

Sexton, F. B. "J. Pinckney Henderson. *The Quarterly of the Texas State Historical Association,* I (January, 1898), pp. 187-203.

Thomas, Frank. "Tequitina! Cradle of Texas." Houston *Post,* (July 1, 1934), no page shown.

Under Texas Skies, I, p. 10 (March, 1951). Austin, Texas: Texas Heritage Foundation Incorporated.

"Wife of First Texas Governor, Mrs. James P. Henderson, Was Woman of Unusual Ability," *Dallas Morning News,* (January 14, 1940).

Winchester, George T. *A Story of Union County and the History of Pleasant Grove Camp Ground.* Privately printed at Mineral Springs, North Carolina (1937).

Index

Abolition, 24
Adams, Edward White (of La.), 104
Adams, John, 5
Adams, Pinckney Henderson, 105
Adjutant-General (State of Texas), 78
Alabama, 71
Alamance, Battle of the, viii
Ampudia, Gen. Pedro de, 87, 88-90
Anderson, Kenneth L., 55, 58, 68, 69, 97
Annexation, 18, 24, 25, 33, 63, 64, 71, 74, 79
Armijo, Gov. (N. Mex.), 91
Atlantic, 22
Attorney General, (Tex. Rep.), 16; State of Tex., 78
Augusta, Ga., 39
Austin Co., Tex., 70
Austin, Moses, 31
Austin, Stephen F., 17
Austin, Tex., ix, 70, 89, 98, 100
Ayish Bayou, 104

Bank of the United States, 39
Barringer, Daniel, 11
Bayard, James H. (of Del.), 99

Baylor, Judge R. E. B., 65, 71; University, x, 71
Bee, Hamilton P., 80
Belgium, King of, 37
Bent's Fort, 91
Bible, the, 50
Biddle, 39, 104
Bishop's Palace, 83
Board of Trade (Brit.), 26
Bonds, Texas, 43
Boone, Daniel, 5
Boonesboro, 5
Boone, Squire, 4
Boundary Act of, 1836, 92
Boutelle, Henry S., vii
Bragg, Braxton, 85
Brazos River, 16
British, 23, 40
Brown, Albert G. (of Miss.), 99
Bryan, Guy (of Tex.), 99
Buchanan, James, 92
Buena Vista, (Battle), 90
Burleson, Gen. Edward, 70, 80
Burnet, David G., 14, 15, 22, 45, 47n, 78
Butler, Gen. Wm. O., 82

Cabarrus, N.C., 11
Cabinet, British, 24
Caithness, 3
Caldwell, Joseph, 11
Calhoun, John C., 64
California, 91
Cameron, Simon (of Pa.), 99
Canning, Geo., 23
Canton, Miss., 13, 14
Capitol (U.S.), 98
Carruth, Elizabeth, 3
Cass, Lewis, 37, 39
Cathedral (Monterrey), 88; Plaza, 85
Cemetery, Congressional, 100; Texas State, 100
Census, (State of Tex.), 94
Chapel Hill College, 10
Chapel Hill, N.C., ix, 45
Chatham Co., Va., 4
Cherokee Grant, 5
Cherokees, 4, 5
Chihuahua, 25
Children (of Henderson), 58; Frances, Julia, Martha
Church of England, 50; Episcopal, 53; First Protestant in Tex., 52; Methodist, 52
Clark, Edward, 65, 80
Clingman, Thomas L. (of N.C.), 99
Coahuila, 32
Columbia, Tex., 17, 51
Commissioner, Gen. Land Off. (State of Tex.), 78
Comptroller, (State of Tex.), 78
Congress, Continental, 5
Congress, Mexican, 31, 32
Congress, (Tex. Rep.), 22, 38, 64, 67-69
Congress, (U.S.), 64, 66, 91-93, 100-104
Conner, J.E., ix
Constitution, Mex. Fed., (1824), 32
Constitution, (State of Tex.), 65
Constitution, (Tex. Rep.), 42, 65
Constitution, U.S., 9, 92
Consular Offices, 43
Convention, Constitutional (Tex.), 65, 66
Convention, Virginia, 5
Cooke, Wm. G., 78

Corpus Christi, 33, 34, 91
Cos, Gen. Martin P. de, 32
Cotesworth, Charles, 3
Cotton, 32, 42, 43
Cox, Frances (Mrs. J. P. Henderson), 49, 50, 51, 58, 103-105
Cox, James, 104
Cox, John, 49, 103
Crawford, viii
Crittenden, John J., (of Ky.), 99
Crump, W. E., 70, 72

Darnell, Nicholas H., 75n, 93
Daughters of the Amer. Rev. (Tyler), 96n
Davis' Bluff, 91
Davis, Col. Jefferson, 85, 87, 98
Debt, public, 77
Declaration of Independence, Am., viii
de Defandis, 30
Democrat, Jeffersonian, 67
De Shields, James T., 6 (quote), 17, 80, 93
Dragoons, Second, 83
Duels, 67
Duffield, Wm. C., 57
Dumfries, 3

East Orange, N.J., 104
East Texas, 53, 63, 68, 95
Education, 65, 66, 78; (see also Schools, public)
England, 22, 24, 29, 35, 38-40
Europe, 18, 21, 22, 36, 39, 49, 104

Fanthorpe, Tex., later Anderson, 70
Federalist, 3, 9
Fitch, Graham N. (of Ind.), 99
Flag, Lone Star, 71, 72
Foote, Sen. Henry S., 14
Fordell, estate of, 2
Ford, John S., 68, 74
Foreign Office, British, 24, 26, 27
Foreign Office, French, 34
Foreign Relations, Com. on (Tex. Rep.), 22
Forsythe (or Forsyth), John, 64
Fowler, Littleton, 52
France, viii, 22, 24, 25, 29, 32, 35, 36, 38, 39, 68

France, King of, 38, 41, 43; (see also Louis Phillipe)
Franco-Texienne Scheme, 47n
Franklin, Benjamin, 23, 46
French, 23, 49, 103
French Embassy Building, (Austin, Tex.), 47n
French Lick, 5
Frontier Battalion, 91
Funeral, state (J. P. Henderson), 98-100

Galveston Bay and Texas Land Co., 55
Galveston, Tex., 50
Garner, N. B., 68
Geisler, Arthur H. (of Okla. City), 105
Gillespie, Capt. R. A., 82
Goliad, 91
Governor (Tex.), 70, 77-81, 86
Granville Co., Va., 4
Granville, Earl of, 4, 27
Great Britain, viii, 22-24, 40
Greek Revival, architecture, 51
Green River, 5
Green, Thomas Jefferson, 15
Greer, John R., 94
Gregg, The Rt. Rev. Alexander, 51
Gulf of Mexico, 77

Hamilton, Gen. James, 23, 39, 40, 41, 42, 44, 47n
Hammond, James H. (of S.C.), 99
Hanover Square, London, 50
Hansford, Judge John M., 68
Harrisburg Co., Tex., later Harris Co., 38, 67
Harris, John W., 78
Harry, John B., 14
Hartford, Conn., 11
Hart, Nathaniel, 4
Hart, Thomas, 4
Harvard, xn
Haskell. Wm. B., 11
Hays, Col. Jack, 80, 84, 86, 91
Hemphill, John, 78
Henderson, Archibald, grandfather of Dr. A. Henderson, 11
Henderson Counties, in Ky., N.C., Tenn., Texas, 6

Henderson, Dr. Archibald of U. of N.C., ix, 11, 21
Henderson, Frances (daughter), 96n, 104
Henderson, James, 3
Henderson, James Pinckney, ancestry, 1-6; Att. Gen., 16; Character and appearance, 53, 56, 68; Childhood and Youth, 1, 9, 10; Diplomacy, 21, 22, 25, 26, 33, 34, 36-38, 40, 42-44, 92; Education, 10, 11; Family, 3, 9, 49-51, 58, 103-105; Funeral, 98-100; Gov., 63, 67, 69, 71, 72, 77, 78, 91; Homes, 6, 9, 13, 50; Inauguration, 70-74; Law practice, 16, 53-55, 58; Military Career, 11, 14, 80, 81, 83, 86, 88, 90; Secretary of State (Tex.), 18; Senator, U.S., 98
Henderson, Judge Richard, 4
Henderson, Lawson, 3, 4, 9, 10
Henderson, Samuel, 2; Children, 2
Henderson, Thomas, 3
Henderson, towns of, 6
Henderson, Wm., 3
Highlands (of Scotland), 1, 2, 3
Hogan, Wm. R., *The Texas Republic*, 50-51
Hogg, James, 2
Hoke vs. Henderson, 3
Horton, Alexander, 68, 70, 75n, 81
Houston, David Franklin, xn
Houston, Nancy, ix
Houston, Sam, viii, 15-17, 23, 25, 36, 37, 42, 55, 57, 64, 77, 98, 100
Humann, 47n
Hunt, Memucan, 15, 22, 27n, 38, 64, 67
Huston, Felix, 15, 47n, 68

Indians, 18, 77, 90, 91; (see also Cherokees)
Invincible, 15
Iredell, N.C., 11
Ireland, 2
Irion, Robt. A., 24, 25, 33, 34, 37

Jackson, Andrew, viii, ix, 47n, 73, 74
Jackson, Andrew, Sr., xn
Jamestown, Va., vii
Jefferson, Thomas, 5

113

Johnston, Albert Sidney, 68
Johnston, Wm., 4
Jones, Anson, 22, 36, 65, 68, 71, 72, 77
Kearney, Brig. Gen. Stephen, 91, 92
Kentucky, County of, 5; State of, 71
Kinney, Henry L., 80
Kitrell, Norman, 55, 69

Lafitte, J. & Co., 47n
Lamar, Gen. Mirabeau Buonaparte, 18, 23, 36, 37, 39, 41, 43, 44, 59, 68, 80, 85, 90, 91, 93, 94
Lancers, Mexican, 83
Laredo, 80, 90, 91, 93
Lawson, Hugh, 3
Lawson, Violet, 3
Law, Spanish, 54; English Common, 54-78
Legislature, (Tex.), 66, 70, 78, 80, 98
Lehigh Coal and Navigation Co., 104
Lexington, Mass., viii
Lieut. Gov. (Tex.), 70, 75n, 81, 94
Linares, Mex., City of, 87
Lincoln Co., N.C., ix, 3, 9
Lincolnton, N.C., ix, 9, 69, 100
Lipscomb, Abner S., 45, 78
Lleano, Don Manuel M., 87
Logan, Miss, 3
London, 24, 41, 45, 50
Lone Star, 9
Louisa Co., 4, 5
Louis Phillipe, King, 33, 43
Lower California, 25
Lutrell, John, 4
Lyman, Gen. Wm. (Mass.), 103
Lyman, Martha, 49
Lynch, James, 59, 65

Macon, Ga., 39
Madison Co., Miss., 13
Marcy, Wm. L., 91
Marshall, Tex., 53, 98
Masonic Lodges, 53
Massachusetts, vii
Matamoros, 34
Mecklenburg Co., N.C., viii
Mexican Federal Republic (1824), 31
Mexico, viii, 15, 16, 18, 23, 24, 26, 29, 30, 33, 34, 54, 64, 77, 79, 80, 87, 89, 92

Militia, N.C. State, Fifth Div., 11
Miller, Dr. James B., 69
Ministers of the Gospel, 65
Mission, Franciscan (San Augustine), 52
Mississippi, 6, 15
Mississippi Rifles, 85
Molé, Count, 30, 31, 34, 35, 37
Monroe, N.C., viii, ix, xn
Monterrey, Battle of, 81-83, 86, 90, 91, 94
Moreno, Col., 86
Morrell, Rev. Wm., 70
Mulattoes, 36
Munson, Ira, 90
Murphy, Gen., 25

McCulloch, Capt. Ben., 82, 84
McDorrett, Gen. A., 12n
McDowell, Gen. A., 11
McIntosh, Gen. Geo., 26, 38, 45
McLendon, Sarah, 53

Nacogdoches, Tex., 16, 52, 53, 55
Nashville, Tenn., 5
Nassau, Duke of, 96n
Navy, Texas, 37
Negroes, 25, 36
New Kent Co., Va., 3
New Mexico, 91, 92
New York, 11
North America, 21
Northampton, Mass., 49
North Carolina, viii, 2, 4-6, 14-16, 23, 100
North Carolina, Univ. of, viii, ix
North, the, 18
Novak, Dr. Edwin, ix
Nuevo Leon, 87

Oakes, Thomas J., 11
Obispado (see Bishop's Palace)
Ocean, (Steamer), 15
O'Connell, 24
Ohio River, 5
Ohio State Univ., ix
"Old Rough and Ready" (see Taylor, Gen. Zachary)
Orange Co., Va., 4
Ordinance of 1787, 91
Oregon, 25, 64
Orizimbo, 16

Ortega, Gen. J. Manuel, 87

Pakenham, 30
Paley, Wm. (quote), 67
Palmerston, Lord, 22, 24, 26, 27, 40, 45
Paris, France, 11, 30, 39, 41, 45, 49
Parsh-Salzburg, Austria, 96n
Pastry War, 46n
Pennsylvania, 11, 104
Phelps, Dr. Orlando, 16
Philadelphia, viii, 5, 49, 103
Piedmont, the, 2
"Pig Incident," 47n
Pinckney, James, 3
Pleasant Retreat Academy, (N.C.), 10
Polk, James K., 64, 66, 92, 93
Pontois, 40, 42
President (U.S.), 92, 98; Tyler, 64, 66; Jackson, 47n, 73, 74; Polk, 64-66, 92, 93
Preuschen, Baron Clemens Von, 96n, 104; Ernst, 96n
"Prissel Baker, Freed Woman," 104
Public Lands, 74n

Queen, (Anne) Submission of Scots, 1
Quitman, John A. (of Miss.), 99

Randall, Mrs. Frances Henderson, ix, 11n
Rangers, Texas, 80, 82-84, 94
Raymond, James H., 78
Ray, Worth S., 3
Reid, David S. (of N.C.), 99
Reid, Samuel, 85
Representatives, House of (Tex. Rep.), 38; State of Tex., 72, 73
Representatives, House of (U.S.), 64, 98, 99
Requeña, Gen. P., 87
Revolution, American, vii
Revolution, July (France), 33
Revolution, Texas, 32
Rhodes Scholar, x
Richard Henderson Company, 4
Rinconada, Pass of the, 87
Rio Grande, 79, 81, 92
Roberts, Gov. O. M., 56

Roberts, Samuel, 41
Robison (of Sabine), 93
Rowan Co., N.C., 3
Rowan, N.C., 11
Rusk, Thomas J., 16, 54, 55, 58, 65, 69, 78, 97, 98; Town of, 53

Sabbath observance (Tex.), 52
St. Cloud, Court of, 22, 23, 46
St. George's Chapel, 50
St. James's, Court of, 22, 46
Saligny, Alphonse de, 34, 35, 37, 38-42, 44, 47n
Salisbury, N.C., 4, 11
San Antonio, 60n
San Augustine, Tex., 50, 51, 52, 54, 55, 56, 58; University, 51; County, 65
San Fernando de Pasos, 87
San Jacinto, Battle of, 15, 18, 32, 85, 88
San Juan de Ulua, 30
San Patricio, Tex., 91
Santa Anna, 15, 16, 30, 31, 32, 88
Santa Catarina River, 84
Saunders, R. C., 39
Schools, public, 66, 78, 79, 93
Scotland, 1, 2, 6
Scots, 1
Secretary of State (Tex. Rep.), 18, 24, 41, 45; State of Tex., 78
Secretary of State (U.S.), Forsythe, Calhoun, Upshur, 64; Buchanan, 92
Secretary of War (U.S.), 92
Senate, (State of Tex.), 70, 73
Senate, (Tex. Rep.), 17, 44, 69, 72
Senate, (U.S.), 64, 78, 98, 100
Seward, Wm. H. (of N.Y.), 99
Sexton, F. B., 53, 56, 57, 65, 67
Shaw, James B., 78
Simmons, James F., (R.I.), 99
Slavery, 24, 25, 42, 104
Smith, Ashbel, 11, 68
Smyth, G. S., 98
Soult, Marshall, 41, 42, 44, 45, 47n
South Carolina, ix, 3, 39, 51
"South Sea," 4
South, the, 13, 25, 38
Spain, King of, 31
Stars and Stripes, 71, 72, 89

115

Star Spangled Banner, 9
Stevenson, 39
Strathaven, 2
Sunday School, Union, 52
Supreme Court, N.C., 10
Supreme Court, U.S., 3, 98; Texas, 78
Sutherland, 2, 3
Sword (gold hilted), 90, 96
Sycamore Shoals, Ky., 5

Tariff, 32, 33, 43, 44, 78
Tarrant, E. H., 65
Taxes, 78, 79, 92
Taylor, Gen. Zachary, 80-82, 85, 87, 90, 91
Terrell, Judge Geo. W., 57
Texas A&M, x
Texas Coll. of Arts and Industries, ix
Texas, Republic of, viii, 15, 16, 18, 21, 22, 23, 25, 26, 29, 31-36, 38, 39, 43, 45, 50, 52, 54, 59, 63, 64, 67, 71, 72, 78, 94
Texas, State of, viii, ix, 6, 11, 13, 14, 77-80, 92, 94
Texas, The Univ. of, xn
Transylvania Co., 4, 5
Trantham, Dr. Henry T., ix
Travis, Wm. B., 68
Treaty (with France), 43-44
Trumbull, Lyman (of Ill.), 99
Tryon, Gov. Wm., 4
Twelve-Mile Creek, viii, xn
Twiggs, Gen. David E., 82, 83
Tyler, John, 64
Tyler, Tex., 96n

Union Co., N.C., viii, ix, xn
United States, viii, 14, 16, 18, 22-24, 35-38, 41, 55, 63, 70, 73, 80, 81, 90-92
Upshur, Abel Parker, 64

Van Zandt, Isaac, 64, 93
Velasco, Tex., 15
Vera Cruz, 15, 30
Versailles, Court of, 23
Virginia, 2, 3
Volunteers, Texas, 80, 86, 87, 90

Waco, Tex., x
Wade, Benjamin F. (of Ohio), 99
Wake Forest Coll., x
Ward, Mathias (of Jefferson, Tex.), 101n
Ward, Thomas W., 78
War, Mexican, 67, 80-91; Creek Indian, 71; Revolutionary (U.S.), 103
Washington, D.C., 22, 64, 98, 100
Washington-on-the-Brazos, Tex., 65
Washington Univ. at St. Louis, xn
Watauga River, 5
Watrous, John C., 55
Wesleyan — Male and Female College (St. Augustine, Tex.), 51
Western Carolinian, 10
West Indies, 24
Wheeler, Royal F., 78
Whitehall, 23
Williams, John, 4, 5
Williamson, Robert M., (Three-Legged Willie), 70
Wilson, Henry (of Mass.), 99
Wilson, Woodrow, xn
Wimberly, Horace Jr., 6n
Wimberly, Mrs. Boyce H., ix
Winchester, Douglas, xn
Winchester, Thomas D., Sr., xn
Woll, Gen., 60n
Wood, Col. G. T., 80, 86, 93
Worth, Brig. Gen. Wm. J., 82-84, 87

Yale, 11
Yellow fever, 94
Yoakum, Tex., ix

LIBRARY OF DAVIDSON COLLEGE

Books on regular loan may be checked out for **two weeks**. Books must be presented at the Circulation Desk in order to be renewed.

A fine of **five cents** a day is charged after date due.

Special books are subject to special regulations at the discretion of library staff.